THE GIFT

THE GIFT

A biographical account of Japanese diplomat, Chiune Sugihara, whose legacy continues to burn brightly through the lives of those who received his Gift of Life.

ANNE HOSHIKO AKABORI

EDU-COMM PLUS

Akabori, Anne.
The Gift | Anne Akabori.
ISBN 0-9649674-9-9

Pre-publication copy
Published by Edu-Comm Plus.

TABLE OF CONTENTS

PREFACE

This preface is essentially also a dedication of this book to the Memory of Hiroki Sugihara, eldest son of Consul Chiune Sugihara. It is dedicated to his memory because this book was only possible because of the motivation, inspiration, encouragement and collaboration that he so generously gave to me to make it all possible. When it was discovered that he did not have long to live, he told me that his wish was to have a biography written about his father. He wanted the information in the book to be based on what he and his family knew about him professionally, and as a father. He was aware that there were many articles and books written about his father based on facts that were derived from information that had been recorded in documents and other sources of information. Hiroki believed that it was important to have a written perspective of his father based on information coming from him and his family. He hoped that by doing so, certain speculations, questions and assumptions, good or bad, written about him in the past, could be put to rest. He hoped that words used to describe his father such as elusive and enigma, would no longer be necessary after reading this book. Of course he also realized that it could just as well raise more questions. However, he believed that sharing the family's point of view would be essentially a good thing and would help to clarify some questions that remain about his father's motives. It was a project that Hiroki wanted me to help him to accomplish because he felt that he was uncomfortable writing in English, since Japanese was his first language. He believed that his perspective was important because it would be one that only a son can know about his father. Before his death, I made my promise to him that I would complete this book for him.

This project was possible because Hiroki and I shared a wonderful friendship and an effective working partnership. Our friendship covered over thirty-five years that began with a chance meeting when I was still a teen-ager until Hiroki's untimely death in the year 2001, at the age of 64. When I first met Hiroki, he had recently come from Japan as a foreign student. He arrived in the United

States soon after completing his education in Japan. He had made the decision to enroll in a college in the city of Sacramento, because the cost of tuition and other educational expenses best fit his limited budget. We met at a social function that we both attended. When we first met, we immediately bonded because we shared common interests and because while he wanted to learn English, I expressed to him my wish to learn Japanese. I believe that I must have been the better teacher because he learned English quite well, while I did not learn very much Japanese then. He often visited our home and talked about his family's life in Eastern Europe. He also often spoke about his father's life in Manchuria. This topic was of particular interest to my father who had studied both Russian and Japanese as a student at Sacramento City College in order to pursue a dream he had as a young man. His dream was to eventually go to Manchuria as an American journalist. Our friendship was the kind of relationship based on mutual interest and it lasted until his passing.

There was a wide gap in our relationship where we did not see each other for a long time. It was while we each worked in our chosen careers and raised our respective families. Eventually, we were reunited and easily resumed our former friendship and enjoyed the same rapport as we did before. We were reunited when Hiroki visited the United States with his mother and family for a short tour sponsored by the Holocaust Oral History Group in San Francisco. The idea for the tour was inspired because many people believed that the story of Chiune Sugihara's life saving mission should be told in the United States. It was also an opportunity to reunite his mother, Yukiko, with survivors of her husband's life saving visas. This tour was also inspired by the great success of the then current block buster film, "Schindler's List." The survivors knew that there was a Sugihara List also and wanted Americans to hear their story. The United States tour and her visit at Town Hall in New York made Hiroki and his mother realize that the survivors and many other people believed that the story was an inspiration and lesson for those individuals not familiar with that period of world history. They also realized that his father's courageous humanitarian acts taught profoundly that, "One man can make a difference." Having just recovered from a life threatening illness, Hiroki made the decision to dedicate the remainder of his life towards keeping his father's legacy alive. Hiroki also regarded it as a way to atone for some of his past indiscretions. Although his father never expressed his disappointment about the problems he caused for his family, Hiroki understood that he forgave him when he accepted his apology, and said, "It could have happened to anyone."

Having had the good fortune to have a long lasting friendship with Hiroki, he was comfortable about asking me to help him with his project to help keep his father's legacy alive. However, because of his status as a citizen of Japan and not an American one, he was allowed to stay in the United States for just a limited time. Being unable to stay for an extended time presented organizational and communication problems. Ironically, his inability to stay in the United States was due to his visa limitations. Initially, I began helping him by translating and re-writing an English version of his mother's best selling memoir, "Inochi no Visa." The Japanese title in English was translated as, "Visas for Life." The experience of working on Yukiko Sugihara's book, gave me an opportunity to learn more about Chiune Sugihara and it inspired me to make the decision and commitment to help Hiroki. Following that project, we began our next collaboration by writing Hiroki's memoir, "Puppe's Story." We successfully sold thousands of our books to people who were eager to learn more about Chiune Sugihara. Hiroki was invited to speak at venues all across the United States. The program's sponsors were educational institutions, religious organizations, private organizations, and various community groups throughout the United States, Canada, and other countries. People responded with great interest and they all seemed eager and curious to hear more about Chiune Sugihara. They were moved to hear how he courageously defied authority by following his conscience, and thereby saved thousands of precious lives. People also enjoyed listening to Hiroki tell about his personal remembrances and about his family's experiences in Eastern Europe. Finally, with the encouragement and help of many supporters, Hiroki decided to create a non-profit foundation whose mission would be to perpetuate his father's legacy. Predictably, the non-profit foundation became known as Visas for Life Foundation. The Foundation was finally established in 1997. Unfortunately, late in the year 2000, while we were visiting Scranton, Pennsylvania, he was diagnosed with cancer. The people of Scranton kindly and generously helped Hiroki get much needed medical attention and advice. He was always grateful for their generosity and never forgot the kindness that was extended to him. Unfortunately, Hiroki could not overcome his cancer and passed away seven months after his diagnosis and four years after the Foundation was established.

After Hiroki was diagnosed with terminal cancer, he decided that he wanted to spend the last six months of his life helping me to begin on our third book project. He spent every minute that he was capable to do so, sharing his remembrances, gathering photos and documents relevant to important facts and events, and telling me anecdotes about his father. He told me every personal bit of information that he could remember about his father. He made sure that I jotted down notes about all the historical facts relevant to his father and pushed himself to remember as much as he could. Each day, we worked together as many hours as was physically possible for him. We went over every detail that he could remember that he believed should be put in the book. While he talked, I typed it all on my computer. I believe and hope to this day that all this work he put into the project helped to distract him from the acute pain that he was continually experiencing. The result of all those hours is this special biography about his father and about some of the people that he rescued. It is essentially

Hiroki's story about his father. I consider the book to be a definitive biography of Chiune Sugihara, as Hiroki had hoped it to be. However, it was never meant to be, nor, should it be considered to be an academically driven biography based on research and investigation. Instead, it is meant to be the biographical account of a father, who became a hero as remembered by his son, Hiroki. Hiroki wanted to share his personal perspective with others so that they would have the opportunity to see Chiune Sugihara from the eyes of his son and family. He realized that only he could know and tell what was to him, the real Chiune Sugihara.

Before Hiroki passed away, we had discussed many different titles for this book. However, while visiting a very supportive descendant of a survivor in Chicago, I had the opportunity to meet his family and his children. It was this meeting with Rick Salomon's children that gave me the inspiration for the title of this book, "The Gift." When I met Rick's lovely children, I realized instantly that they were there with me that day because Chiune Sugihara had saved their grandfather's life by issuing him a life saving visa. But I also realized that the lovely two children sitting next to me were also Chiune's gifts. They were definitely gifts to their parents and family, but I also saw them as gifts to all of us because of the promise that their lives seemed to hold for the future. I also realized that personally, there have been so many gifts in my life since I became involved with the Sugihara story. I received the gift of getting first hand knowledge about the Sugihara Family and their experiences. My appreciation of Chiune Sugihara's legacy is a gift that continues to evolve everyday. I received the gift of meeting many wonderful people because of my involvement in the Foundation. Sugihara's gift of life is truly a testimony and a legacy to those who survive because of him. The fact that his legacy will continue to live through the lives of young people like my friend, Rick's children, is another kind of gift. Hiroki's friendship was a gift. The opportunity to work on this book is a gift.

What could be a more appropriate title for this book! I believe that Hiroki would have understood perfectly the meaning of such a title. Chiune Sugihara never wanted attention about what he did and for the most part tried to remain anonymous. However, I believe, without any doubt, that if he were to meet the children and descendants of those survivors, Chiune would not be able to hide his joy. It is my great hope that those who read this book will learn a little about something that happened in a distant and historical past. I hope they will learn a little about what it takes to think about others before thinking about self. I hope that the stories of each of the survivors will teach a lesson about the strength of character that it took to be a survivor. I hope that readers will understand how profound Chiune's statement was when he said, "Any decent person would have done what I did." Ultimately, it is hoped that everyone who reads this story will learn that gifts that are given with love and kindness will live forever if the recipients remember to appreciate it.

ACKNOWLEDGEMENTS

Without Hiroki's and his mother, Yukiko's collaboration, this book would not have been possible. Chiaki, the second son of Chiune who now oversees the care of his mother, Yukiko, also collaborated with me and provided me with his cooperation and with special insights about his father. Yukiko's generosity in allowing the use of her family photo that was provided to me by Hiroki, should be specially noted. The photos were invaluable because it helped to enhance and lend veracity to the Sugihara family's saga.

I would also like to thank all the people who helped with the physical and mechanical aspects of this project. Without the technical advice that was given to me about how to be more efficient in the use of my outdated computer, by my dear friends, June and Stan Hayashi and my webmaster, Pat Masuda, the project would have been delayed by months.

Translation into English of Chiune's Japanese documents, books and the films that were provided to me by Hiroki was essential for me in order to get a better understanding of what Chiune had said or written. Also the interpretations of sources from the Japanese media when Chiune was interviewed during rare occasions were essential elements that were needed to complete my understanding of what was said or written in Japanese. After Hiroki passed away, I was fortunate to get the cooperation and interest of Mr. & Mrs. Kazuo Masuno, who are very articulate in Japanese as well as English. Their interpretations were an invaluable source of information that filled the void left by Hiroki's passing. I thank them for the hours that they spent with me as we discussed articles written in Japanese.

I want to thank Jane and George Matsuoka who were always there for me by providing any kind of help that was necessary that was directly or indirectly connected with writing this book. I also want to thank Jane for going over the book with her proofreading skills.

Of course the cooperation, interest, and support from all of the survivors and descendants need to be recognized. Their participation and contributions to the Sugihara saga added dimension to the story. Because of their cooperation and generosity by giving of their time, it enabled the story to be told from both sides of the fence. Therefore, my thank yous to George Liebert, Rabbi Graudenz and his daughter Debby, Leo Melamed and the cooperation of his secretary, Patricia Reiffel, and the sons of Bernard and Abram Salomon, Rick and Joe.

I thank my loving husband, Jack, for all the years that he has supported me with his patience, and encouragement. He always showed his interest in my projects by allowing me to feel that my work was also one of his priorities and I will always be grateful for his interest and help.

I thank all the participants who took the time to read my unedited manuscript and sent their thoughts and testimony to me. Their names and quotes are listed on the back cover of the book.

I also believe that in some mysterious way, Hiroki is also grateful for the help that was provided to me so that our project has finally come to fruition.

INTRODUCTION

Everyone likes to receive and to give a gift because it makes both the recipient and the giver happy. A gift is special. There are many kinds of gifts. Some gifts are small but sentimental. Others are extravagant and sometimes very costly. Some gifts are given spontaneously, and others are given with a lot of thought and care. This story is about a most precious gift that was given with love, thought, and courage. The giver of this gift was an obscure Japanese diplomat whose name was Chiune Sugihara. It is a story about a man who considered himself to be an ordinary man and strove to be a decent human being. He was a quiet and humble man who was consistently compelled by his sympathetic nature to help those in need. His priceless gift was the gift of LIFE. The recipients of his gift were Jewish refugees, who were desperately attempting to escape the certainty of imprisonment or death, during a time referred to as the Holocaust. As a result of his precious gift, it is estimated that over 100,000 survivors and their descendants live today. In fact, it was discovered in 1968, 28 years after the deed was done, that he was responsible for saving thousands of lives. Upon this discovery and revelation, he shunned and discouraged any attention that was given to him and simply said, "Any decent person would have done what I did." As the numbers of descendants of survivors continue to grow exponentially, we remember the ancient Jewish proverb: "If you save one life, it is as though you save the world entire."

This is a most wondrous story because it is made up of many little miracles that grew into great and big miracles. This story will be told by highlighting the many little miracles that were threaded within the fabric of Chiune's life. It is a story that is most fitting during Hannukah because it is a story that is filled with many little miracles. It is also a story that should never be forgotten because of its many redeeming values. It is a story that illustrates that despite the evil and darkness that existed during a terrible time, people miraculously held tenaciously to their faith and did not abandon G_D. The recipients of this precious gift became and are today the living testimony and legacy of the "givers" of this precious gift.

These recipients have the responsibility of remembering and appreciating this priceless legacy. The word "givers" was used here because there were other saviors or givers of life, like Sugihara, that are also honored and remembered today. However, this story is about Vice Consul Chiune Sugihara, who was given the honor of being one of the Righteous among the Nations. This account of his life will also include the amazing stories of some of the heroic individuals who received Chiune Sugihara's priceless gift of life.

PART I: BEGINNINGS (1900-1917)

CHIUNE'S EARLY LIFE AND INFLUENCES

"Of ancient race by birth, but nobler yet in his own worth."
John Dryden

To better appreciate the enormity of this story about giving and receiving, we start at the beginning. Appropriately, the story begins with one of those many little miracles, his birthday. His day of birth was considered to be an auspicious one. He was born on a cold, winter morning on January 1, 1900. It was the first day of a new century. His birthplace was in Yaotsu Town, a small village in a remote area of Gifu Prefecture. He was the second son of the family of Yoshimizu and Yatsu Sugihara. It was as though his birth heralded a new century marking the old revitalized with the new. It seemed to point to a destiny that Chiune would be an integral participant of the new century.

According to the Gregorian calendar, his day of birth was January 1, 1900. However, the Japanese have another criterion upon which they base one's day of birth. The Japanese dating system is based on the name of the reigning living emperor. Chiune was born on the 33rd year of the reign of Emperor Meiji. According to the Japanese timetable, his date of birth would be designated as Meiji-33; in other words, the 33rd year of the reign of Emperor Meiji. The Meiji period is considered to be the beginning of the industrial and technological renaissance of Japan. It was a dynamic time with the introduction of industrialization into a nation that was basically an agrarian society. In a relatively short time, Japan had grown into a world industrial power and also developed a formidable naval presence in Asia. All of this gave rise to a sense of pride and nationalism among the people. Four years after Chiune's birth, 1904, Japan defeated Russia in the Russo-Japanese war. As a result of the euphoria due to what was basically a naval victory over Russia, attitudes of confidence and optimism grew about themselves as a people as well as national pride for their country. It is within the context of this kind of optimism and hopes for the future that Chiune was nurtured as a child and his confident outlook reflected the spirit of the times.

HIS BIRTHPLACE

"Every man carries with him the world in which he must live."
Francis Marion Crawford

The story of how the family came to be in Yaotsu is an interesting story that has been handed down through the generations. As one approaches the valley of Yaotsu, the sight of verdant green covering the landscape will be breathtaking. Eventually, you will see the silver thread of the Kiso River meandering through the lush hills and valleys. It is a true panoramic feast for the eyes. However, this scenic beauty only masks the harsh severity of the land where only the majestic, strong, straight and indigenous cedar trees survive. Beneath the tall cedars grow the tenacious and prolific bamboo plants that provide ground cover. There, the winters are extremely harsh and cold. Despite the piercing cold, snow is very rare because as one looks northward, the high mountains effectively block the snow clouds. Only the blasts of arctic winds reach into the valley. To live in such a harsh environment was not by choice but because of necessity. During feudalistic times, the family of his mother, who were samurai, served as retainers for a feudal lord in the special guard unit. Upon their defeat by an opposing lord, it became necessary for the clan to disband and to disperse. Seeking havens of safety, the clan was forced to hide in remote areas not conducive to farming. Capture by the aggressors would have meant certain death. Yaotsu was a perfect place of refuge. The hills and valleys were well covered by the natural vegetation indigenous to the area providing ample hiding places. Survival in such a place was a challenge that could be met by only the most fit. One could only eke out a living at the barest subsistence level and one had to be endowed with great stamina and tenacity in order to endure all the hardships for survival. Miraculously, they survived, and today remnants of the clan continue to farm on terraced land covered by coarse soil. Being descended from such hardy stock was a likely factor that enabled Chiune to meet the challenges that he faced later in life.

Recently, a question arose concerning his place of birth. The controversy was due to the existence of records indicating registration in a town near Yaotsu. The town in question was Kazucho, a neighboring town. It was discovered that his father did indeed register his birth at Kazucho because it was a matter of convenience. His father's place of business as tax officer happened to be in that town. However, within the ten days given to rectify the registration, he properly registered him in Yaotsu. This fact is also in accordance with family accounts that he was born in his mother's family farmhouse in Yaotsu.

HIS NAME

"A good name is rather to be chosen than great riches."
Proverbs 22:1

The next factor that can be considered another miracle is Chiune's name. His father, Yoshimizu was considered a shrewd and practical businessman who had a tendency to be somewhat of a Bon Vivant. He was quick to appreciate the new western ways that were slowly coming to the rural town of Yaotsu. In fact it was said that he was one of the first to acquire and dress in western attire in that area. One would not usually expect that a man of his nature would create the kind of name that he devised for his second-born son. The reason it can be said the name was created is because the name Chiune was practically non-existent in those days. It will forever remain a mystery as to how Yoshimizu Sugihara received the inspiration and vision to name his newly born son so appropriately. When one breaks down the Chinese character of this name, it translates to one thousand (Chi) and new growth (une), such as a new plant. In Japanese, one thousand can refer to mean an infinite number and une can be implied to mean new life. When it is translated, Chiune means, "an infinite number of new lives." The amazing story of his name continues. The surname, Sugihara, was not his father's original name. For whatever reason Yoshimizu decided to change his name, the fact is that it became Sugihara. The interesting thing about the name Sugihara is that it translates to mean cedar grove. Because cedars are of special significance to Jewish lore and regarded as a symbol of courage and strength, the name is a fitting one. As a result, Chiune Sugihara's complete name can mean when translated as one thousand new lives from the family of cedar grove. In Japanese culture, it is considered that one's name becomes an imprint of ones character, so the selection of a name is taken very seriously. One can easily believe that the selection of his name could be considered as amazing or miraculous.

There is another curiosity about his name that was told by a Jewish scholar. It is that when his name is broken down phonetically, the phonetic components of his name connotes rebirth or the promise of new life. Students and followers of the Kabbala would appreciate the threads of mysticism that seem to appear consistently in his life. Mysteries abound in this life, but in the case of Chiune, we know that he had a propensity to be connected with renewal, hope, saving of lives and ultimately, guaranteeing the continuation of life. Perhaps he had a preordained destiny.

(left) Chiune, standing, with two younger brothers. Circa 1914. (right) Yatsu Sugihara, Chiune's mother with four of her sons. Chiune is standing on the left.

HIS FAMILY

"Blessed influence of one true loving human soul on another."
George Eliot

The next special factor that can be considered as very special in his life is the fact that he was blessed with a wonderful mother whom he loved most dearly. It was she who most influenced his character and his world-view. His mother was regarded as the town beauty. In fact she was also highly admired by the people of the town for her refined manners, kindly demeanor and intelligence. Among all of her children, Chiune most closely resembled her because he had inherited her refined classical features. He also spent the most time with her discussing philosophy, literature, and listening to her stories of long ago. However, the most important trait that influenced Chiune was her spiritual nature. She was descended from samurai class as mentioned earlier, and taught young Chiune the way of the Bushi or warrior. She encouraged him to work each day towards trying to reach his highest potential both physically and mentally. She reminded him to care for and strengthen his body each day by exercising and eating well. She encouraged him to hone his mental skills by appreciating and learning something new each day. Fortunately, for Chiune, it was discovered that he had a phenomenal memory referred to as photographic memory. She told him about the importance of maintaining physical cleanliness and mental

Chiune's father, Yoshimiza, who had high hopes that his son would become a doctor.

clarity. Most importantly, his mother emphasized that all of those lessons about physical and mental development that he was reminded about each day were secondary to his spiritual development. She said that he must always continue to strive towards higher spiritual development. She imbued in him an appreciation of life and taught him the Japanese concept of "Okagesama de." It is difficult to accurately translate this idea, but in essence, it meant that life is a gift that must be appreciated. In order to show appreciation, one must cherish and treat their lives with dignity and respect along with the knowledge that all that exists today is a result of what occurred in the past. In other words, the expression referred to the fact that one's life became a possibility only because of the actions of those who existed before us. His mother emphasized that because people in the past had succeeded in living in ways that insured the continuation of our present lives, his responsibility was to strive to live in a way that would insure the continuation of this wonderful legacy for the future generations to come.

It is obvious that Chiune learned this lesson well because he consistently showed concern for humanity throughout his life. He also learned about the philosophy of the true Bushi (samurai warrior), "Hagakure Spirit." Hagakure spirit was the will and knowledge about how to live well and about how to face death. It was considered that one died well if they lived well, or if they gave up their life for a cause that one strongly believed was a just cause.

He was always deeply sensitive about his mother's frail health and consistently returned from school as early as possible in order to help her with her chores. Upon his return from school, he helped to care for his younger siblings, helped his mother with her chores, and took the responsibility of sweeping the soot that piled up in their yard and doorsteps every day. Because their house was near the railroad tracks where the trains passing by each day were fueled by coal, this chore was a daily routine for Chiune. However, watching the trains go by each day also sparked his imagination and inspired him to have dreams of traveling to faraway lands and the desire to learn about exotic people and places. In fact, living near the tracks helped to develop his life long fascination about travel and about trains.

It was also during this time that Japan had developed a network of sophisticated rail lines that connected the small towns, villages, and hamlets. Telegraph lines were connected to the remotest areas. Advances in communication whetted Chiune's curiosity for more information and about distant places and he dreamed about faraway lands. His hope was to someday travel abroad and to experience being in different countries. He desired to meet people of different cultures. His greatest hope was to someday visit America and he made the decision to learn English. Trains really became a fascination for him, and ironically, trains eventually later played a big part in his life.

His father was a practical businessman and was ahead of his time. He understood the value of education and encouraged his children to continue their educational career beyond high school. He was not only a good businessman, but was also an innovative entrepreneur. Some described him as being flamboyant in his manner and dress. He also managed to marry the town beauty. His job made it necessary for the family to move several times before they settled in Nagoya City for a relatively extended period of time. He was the father of six children, five sons and a daughter. To his credit, four of his six children all attended college. This was regarded as quite amazing for that time because it was very rare for any children from middle class families to go to college after graduating from high school.

Yoshimizu's family history is somewhat unclear. Before he acquired the name Sugihara, his original surname was Iwai. Iwai is a name comparable to Smith in the United States. It seemed that over half the population in the particular town where he lived was named Iwai. This caused problems such as confusion in mail delivery. Being a practical person, he may have decided upon a more distinctive name in order to avoid mail delivery delays. Another theory is that he may have changed his name to that of a benefactor that he had greatly admired. This brief portrayal of his family indicates that Chiune was blessed in early life with good parents, a happy family, excellent mental and physical health, but most of all, a loving and respectful relationship with his mother.

HIS EARLY EDUCATION

"Education commences at the mother's knee, and every word hearsay of little children tends toward the formation of character."
Hosea Ballou

"Education makes people easy to lead, but difficult to drive; easy to govern, but impossible to enslave." General Omar Bradley

His educational paths lead him well towards his destiny. All of the incidences and events that determined which school he would attend, consistently were synchronized in such a way that he went to just the right school that best prepared him for his life's work. This mysterious synchrony of his educational career can be considered in the category of a miracle because it all turned out so well for him to prepare him for the future.

The first school that he attended was in the town of Kuwano in Gifu Prefecture. After a very brief time in Kuwano, the family moved to Nakatsu where he also attended school for a short duration. Finally, when they moved to Nagoya City, he stayed there until his high school graduation. In Nagoya, he attended Furuwatari Elementary School. There he excelled academically and received high honors in citizenship and deportment. Records still exist attesting to his excellent grades, perfect attendance, and impeccable citizenship. To receive the highest commendations was reward enough, however, to receive it from Furuwatari School was regarded as an accomplishment of the highest degree because that school was one of the most prestigious schools in that area. In order to be accepted at Furuwatari School, students were required to pass stringent examinations. As mentioned previously, Chiune had a phenomenal memory. His routine was to memorize everything that was taught each day so that he would not have to do homework. This extra time provided him the time to help his mother. He walked to school and back each day; a total of approximately four miles a day. He happily accepted his daily routine and regarded his daily walks as beneficial for strengthening his legs. It is probably due to these daily walks, jogs and runs that he became one of the fastest runners in the school. His forte was the 100 meter race. He also loved baseball and remained a devoted fan of the game.

Some of his contemporaries remembered him for his eccentric behavior. For example, he would be seen walking through the school corridors with a string looped around his head. The string would be looped around both of his ears. Hanging on one end of the string would be a bottle of ink, and hanging on the other end would be his pen. When asked why he carried his school equipment in that way, he answered, "I want to be sure that I would not lose them and always have it on hand in case I need to take notes." The irony of the situation was the fact that it was well known among the students that he was the brilliant student who never needed to write down any notes because of his ability to commit to memory anything that he had read or heard. Some even considered him eccentric because he was diligent about going straight home when school was dismissed. They did not realize that he went home only because of his concern for his mother. He wanted get back as soon as possible so that he could help her with her chores.

During the hot summer months during summer break, most of Chiune's time was spent helping to work on his grandparent's rice farm in Yaotsu. It was back breaking labor but the experience did help to strengthen his stamina. He had already inherited the large bones, broad upper body, and relatively short sturdy legs, that was not considered proportionate to his long sturdy trunk. Hiroki, his eldest son, often remarked in jest that their body makeup was an important attribute for samurai in the guard unit. He would say, "Our sturdy short legs enabled us to be immovable objects." It was a predominant trait found among the males in the Sugihara family and it even became evident in his children when he became a father. The physical labor experienced on those hot summer days also eventually proved to be a positive factor in his later life.

On those long hot summer days, when work on the fields was completed, he and his brothers would go to the banks of the Kiso River to cool off by fishing and swimming until dark. By this time, he had four brothers, one older and three younger. Chiune never forgot those idyllic times that he spent with his brothers. He also enjoyed watching all the ships, boats and freighters making their way towards Nagoya or going to the more remote rural areas. The River Kiso was an important waterway for commerce and travel. It was a river that flowed to the Pacific Ocean. Throughout the day, there was always much activity on those waters. Chiune found all of the activities on the river quite fascinating, and more than likely, it whetted and increased his already developed appetite for travel.

After matriculating from Furuwatari School, Chiune was accepted at Nagoya Prefecture Daigo Chu, another prestigious school with very high standards. He was consistent in maintaining his characteristic academic excellence and was again the top student at the school. When he enrolled at Nagoya Daigo Chu, Emperor Meiji passed away. It was the end of the Meiji Period. The new era was named after the next emperor, Yoshihito Taisho and became known as the Taisho Period. This was the year 1912, and Chiune was twelve years old. In 1916, just before Chiune was about to graduate from that school, his father was transferred to an office in an outpost in Korea. Korea was annexed to Japan in 1910 and was under Japanese control. The timing was quite disconcerting for Chiune because it was just a few months before his graduation. The decision was made that he would stay in Nagoya himself until he graduated. A small room was rented and he successfully graduated from Nagoya Daigo Chu at the top of the class with high honors.

After his graduation, Chiune looked forward to going to Korea to be reunited with his family. The family joyfully celebrated his return and congratulated him for the high honors that he received upon his completion of high school. He discovered that his father, the entrepreneur that he was, had purchased property that was a hotel. It was a hotel primarily for businessmen and it promised to become a very lucrative enterprise. However, Chiune was quite dismayed at this turn of events because he observed that his mother's responsibilities had increased twofold. Proprietorship of a hotel increased her daily chores. Along with her regular chore of keeping up the household, she now had the responsibility of also running a hotel. To his consternation, he noticed that her physical and mental pressures increased with her new responsibilities. He was alarmed because he observed that it was beginning to take a toll on her health. As a result, he tried to help her as much as he was able to by assuming as much of her chores that he could possibly take over. Just as he had done as a young man in Nagoya, he tried to do whatever he could to help alleviate her workload.

In the meantime, his father was busy making plans for his acceptance and enrollment at a nearby prestigious medical school, Keijoo Medical University, in Seoul, Korea. Yoshimize was completely insensitive to the hopes and dreams of his son Chiune, his most academically accomplished and capable son. He was happily developing his own plans towards realizing his own hopes for his son's future.

HIS DECISION

"This is the thing that I was born to do."
Samuel Daniel

This next event is considered as a small miracle because it was something so unexpected of Chiune, who was considered a model son. Everyone considered him to be the ideal son because he was always responsible, helpful, a good student, and respected the authority of his father. One of the most important traits for a Japanese son or daughter was to show respect for parents, referred to as filial piety. Chiune never disappointed his father and was a source of pride for his family because of his impeccable character and academic accomplishments. However, at the age of seventeen, he did something that would have been regarded as unthinkable for someone like Chiune.

As stated previously, his father, Yoshimizu, had always expressed the hope that Chiune would become a medical doctor. He spoke of it often and was planning his educational career confident in the fact that Chiune would be qualified to enter any of the best schools of that time because of his impeccable academic accomplishments. Chiune was reluctant to disappoint his father or to even go against his wishes, so he was never able to express to him his personal desire to learn languages, especially English. His father was not aware of his desire to go to a University to learn to be a language teacher. In fact, Chiune felt that his father was quite unreasonable about his becoming a doctor, because his father knew how much he disliked the sight of blood. However, the day finally came when it was time to take the entrance examination to enter medical school. His father had made all of the prior arrangements.

Chiune, circa 1918, before he left his home to live in Tokyo.

Young Chiune dutifully set off for the appointed examination. His mind was in turmoil about what to do. If he took the examination, his future would be predictable. He would complete his education and would most probably be a doctor in a town such as Nagoya, where the family had lived. It was in Nagoya, Aichi Prefecture, that Chiune had gone to school until his high school graduation. In his heart of hearts, he knew that such a future was not the one that he desired. He knew that he wanted to learn languages, teach languages and hoped to travel. He wanted to discover worlds outside of Japan. As he prepared to take the test, he was overcome with emotion. He thought about how much his father had done for him and realized that he was really looking after his best interest. It will never be known how Chiune came up with his decision and the amount of courage it took to follow his own conviction about what was best for him and his life. Until now, he had always been a dutiful son who always obeyed the wishes of his father. Once his decision had been made, Chiune, wrote his name on the examination paper to show that he had been there and left without taking the test. Chiune realized what the consequences of his act of outright disobedience would be and was prepared to face those consequences.

When notice of his son's acceptance to the medical school did not arrive, Yoshimizu set out to find out what may have happened. It did not take long for him to realize that this son, for whom he had the highest of expectations, had purposely failed to take the test. As a father, in that period of time in Japan, he had no alternative but to tell his son that his disobedience meant that as his father, he would have no further obligations to him. Chiune was prepared to face the consequences.

HIS DEPARTURE

"I have lost all and found myself."
John Clark

"Onobori-san" (country bumpkin journeys to the capital)
A Japanese expression

The day of his departure to Tokyo was a day that Chiune always remembered with sadness. As he parted from his mother, she gave him all of the money that she had been saving for an emergency. He declined to accept her gift because he realized how long she had been saving it, but she insisted. His father, Yoshimizu, still suffering the wounds of his disappointment refrained from seeing him off. Instead, he sent his younger brother, Otowa, to give him a message and packets of sugar. In 1918, sugar was very scarce and was considered to be a very valuable commodity. The note from his father instructed him to bring the gift of sugar to a friend in Tokyo. He advised him that this colleague would be able to help him and to give him introductions to others who would be able to help him to make adjustments necessary to survive in the big city of Tokyo. This was a very touching gesture from a father whose pride was hurt and was still feeling the pain of what he considered a betrayal by his son. As the train pulled away, the deep sadness that he felt as he saw his mother standing at the platform, was somewhat lifted when he received his father's message delivered by Otowa. He realized that he was leaving with blessings of success from both of his parents. This was the scene of Chiune's departure and it was also the beginning of a new phase of his life. Little did Chiune realize that his decision to not become a doctor, would in the future, prove to lead him to a time and place where he would be responsible for saving more lives than he could ever have saved as a doctor.

PART II: HIS EDUCATION (1918-1924)

WASEDA UNIVERSITY

"The man who graduates today and stops learning tomorrow is uneducated the day after." Newton Diehl Baker

Another miracle took place concerning his choice of school. Of all the universities and colleges that he could have attended, Chiune's fate was to enroll at Waseda University. The circumstances were such that it was the only school that would accept him. The enrollment periods for most of the other universities had passed by the time he was settled in Tokyo. As luck would have it, Waseda University was one of the few that accepted late enrollment. It was a school that was considered to be philosophically and educationally progressive. The founder of the school was Shigenobu Okuma. He was considered to be one of the foremost progressive thinkers of that time. The motto of the school stated, "Serve the People." Okuma believed that the purpose of a good education was to enable one to reach one's highest ideal. That ideal was to serve the people. Serving the people required that one must listen well to the voice of the people and to act accordingly. Okuma taught that when one served his people, one was in essence contributing to his community, country, and to society. At that time, the concept of service to the community and its people was a relatively new one in Japan. It was still a country working towards shedding its centuries-old authoritarian and feudalistic ideas of government into one that advocated for democratic ideals. But it was an idea that inspired Chiune and he embraced its merits. Along with advocating for progressive social views, Waseda University also had a very excellent English department.

When Chiune first stepped foot in Tokyo, he was overwhelmed by the hustle and bustle of the big city. Although Nagoya was considered a city, Tokyo was so much bigger and he had never seen so many people in one place. He was intimidated by the fast pace of life and the fact that everyone seemed to be hurrying to some designated destination. As confused as he was, he managed to find a modest rooming house in which to spend the night. Eventually, he was settled and had to find the school that would accept him. As luck would have it, that school was Waseda

University. He immediately began making plans about how to support himself as well as to find a way to pay for his educational expenses.

He realized that the first thing that he must do was to find a job. He took any odd job that he was able to find in order to pay for all of his expenses. His jobs ranged from being a delivery person, salesman, and during the school breaks, he even worked as a longshoreman at Tokyo Bay. Having developed physical strength and agility during his youth, he easily took on the challenges required of this very physical job. What he liked most about this job was that it paid well and he was able to save a little for the coming semester. He continued to go to school and always took the maximum units. He usually had two part time jobs. In order to keep his expenses down, he discovered the best second hand bookstores to make his book purchases. Despite his impoverished status, he was always a top student. He survived by living in modest living quarters and he economized in every way possible. Due to the experiences of his Waseda days, his frugal habits remained with him for the rest of his life. The daily challenges that he met, helped him to realize that he was capable of surviving on his own and he never regretted that he had listened to his heart. The relationship between him and his father had improved because Yoshimizu had slowly and gradually accepted his son's decision. Chiune only regretted that he was so far from his mother and could not be around to help her and to talk with her. However, he faithfully continued to write to her and told her all the news about his many experiences at Waseda University.

Chiune continued to excel in all of his classes. In order to improve his English language skills, his habit was to go to the school library to read the American and English newspapers whenever possible. He usually liked reading articles in the London Times and the American publication, The Daily Mail. He also took advantage of every opportunity to strike up conversations with foreign students whose first language was English. These conversations with them helped him to improve his pronunciation and listening skills. It didn't take long for his instructors to recognize his excellence and command of English. He was soon elevated to a position as part time tutor at the school. Interestingly enough, at the same time that he was enrolled, there was another brilliant English student named Kyohei Hagiwara. He later became the foremost English expert and textbook writer in Japan.

What happened during his second year at Waseda University can be considered as another important miracle. His being there was the beginning of what would lead him to an unexpected series of events that eventually changed his life forever. Chiune had been struggling for over a year trying to make ends meet and at the same time maintain his excellent grades. By now, he had the reputation as being the top English language student in the school and as mentioned previously, was hired as a tutor. It was at about this time that an unfortunate and serious economic setback occurred. A printing firm who had hired him part time, found themselves in financial difficulty. So one night, they secretly left in the middle of the night and took whatever they could carry out and fled the premises. As a result, Chiune was never paid for his weeks of work. He had been depending on those wages to pay for his expenses for that month. These kinds of setbacks made it clear to Chiune that he must find a way to improve his current situation. Adding to his already difficult situation was the fact that he had recently invited his younger brother, Otowa, to come to live with him. Therefore, his expenses had increased just before the economic setback occurred. Otowa had eagerly accepted his invitation and was enrolled at Meiji University. Chiune realized the necessity for him to improve his economic condition, so he began to explore different options.

One day, during this economically troubling time, Chiune's attention was drawn to a sign posted in the school lounge near the library. It was an article written in the newspaper, Osaka Shimpo. It was an ad that advertised for potential candidates who met qualifications to apply for a generous scholarship. Students able to meet the requirements and to pass the tests would be eligible for this generous offer. It was offered to students interested in enrolling at the Japanese Foreign Ministry School of Harbin Gakuin University at Harbin, Manchuria. The recruitment notice was posted by the Japanese Foreign Office. The scholarship promised that candidates who met the qualifications and passed the tests would get complete training, with full tuition, room and board, as well as an extra stipend for personal expenses. For Chiune, who presently was suffering serious financial setbacks, this announcement was an incredible one. He quickly jotted down the necessary information and went directly to the office where he would be able to get the application and the information needed to be eligible.

He was encouraged when he discovered that he met all the basic requirements. However, the problem of passing all the tests was a challenge for anyone, including a person that was as gifted as Chiune. The usual candidate took at least two to three years of preparation and training in order to be able to pass this extremely difficult test. According to the scheduled date for the test, Chiune realized that he had less than two months to prepare for the test. The day that he checked about the test requirements in a publication published by the government was May 24, 1919, and the test was scheduled for July 3, 1919. He was determined not to be discouraged because he did not want to lose the rare opportunity to possibly be accepted for this incredible scholarship and he began to prepare for his next step.

THE CHALLENGE

"The bravest sight in the world is a man fighting against odds."
Franklin Knight Lane

The average person probably would not seriously consider facing the seemingly insurmountable challenges that Chiune faced in deciding to take the test. However, Chiune confidently began to devise his game plan in an objective manner.

Chiune, circa 1920, before he embarked upon his new life in Manchuria.

In order to pass the tests, he would have to have a comprehensive knowledge of international law, civil law, economics, world history, and have great command of a foreign language. Chiune was determined to take on this challenge and he began planning his strategy. He realized that his lack of time was his biggest obstacle.

He also knew that he would not have to be too concerned about the foreign language portion of the test because he was confident about his English ability. His plan included getting all the books he would need pertaining to each test subject at the local second hand bookstore and he developed for himself efficient study methods that would be effective for him.

Many years later he was asked to write a manual about how to pass a test. The name of the essay was, "Yuki no Harbin Yori." Translated into English, it reads, A Letter from Harbin on a Snowy Day." Because it was a well known fact that Chiune was the youngest applicant to pass the Foreign Ministry test, his accomplishments had elevated him to celebrity status. The new and younger students considered him a folk hero. His article was regarded as the bible of study guides. In the article, he wrote about his personal ideas and listed his study tips. His first recommendation was that students should refine their foreign language reading and understanding skills because by doing so, it would help them to expand their intellectual base. He emphasized that in order to improve in foreign language skills, one must regularly read periodicals and newspapers. He also wrote that it was essential to keep up with current events by reading them in their foreign language choice. He stated that making a habit of reading current event periodicals, increased one's vocabulary in that language and would also help improve understanding of law, economics and history. He considered that increasing one's vocabulary was not only important, but also basic. When shortage of time was a factor, he recommended that students analyze the meanings of words by the context of the material rather than looking up each word in the dictionary. He also emphasized the importance of understanding and attaining mastery of grammar and word structure. He also recommended using word analysis or understanding the properties of words such as prefixes, suffixes, and root words. There was one particular advice that he did not highly recommend and stressed that it was to be utilized only when faced with severe limitation of time. He said that instead of reading the complete book, read the beginning, middle, and end and to try to understand the main points so that most of the important points would be most likely covered. His treatise on how to take a test revealed a few of his personal traits. It showed him to be an astute person who had pragmatic tendencies. Miraculously, his strategies served him well and he successfully accomplished the "impossible." The fact that he was able to accomplish the almost impossible task of passing the tests with so little time for studying was truly one of those small miracles that seemed to appear periodically throughout his life.

According to test score results that were later posted, his was not the top or the lowest score, but he scored right in the middle. This episode of his life clearly illustrated that he possessed the admirable characteristics needed for leadership. Passing the examination illustrated his determination, perseverance, intelligence and steadfastness. Upon receiving his scholarship and his acceptance to Harbin Gakuin, there were many more important new decisions that he would have to make as he faced another chapter in his life.

HARBIN GAKUIN

"Learning is like rowing upstream, not to advance is to drop back."
Chinese proverb

"Sumeba Miyako" (Where one lives, one comes to love.)
Japanese expression

The next decision that faced Chiune and what determined how his decision was made was an interesting series of events that can be considered as being miraculous. As stated previously, according to results of the test scores taken by all the candidates, Chiune's score was not the highest or the lowest, but a median score. That fact deprived him of the opportunity to have first choice in his foreign language selection at Harbin Gakuin. It happened that the most popular language of choice at that time was English and it had already been chosen by the highest scoring students. Therefore, he did not have the option to choose English. Spanish was the second most popular language. Therefore, Spanish was a language that had already been chosen by second place students. He realized that the two languages that he had most hoped to choose were not available to him. His predicament was to decide which language to choose other than the ones that he had hoped to choose. He understood that he had an important decision to make and needed to think very carefully about what his selection would be.

Chiune had been mulling over the possibilities of his language choice, when he happened to get involved in a casual conversation with a friendly and loquacious elderly officer in the ministerial office. It happened that this talkative officer was one of the managers in the personnel office. During the course of their conversation, the officer began to tell Chiune about his many years of service in the foreign ministry. He shared his opinions about the current conditions within the ministry and bragged about his vast experience due to his long years of service. When Chiune revealed to him his dilemma about making a choice for his language selection, the old officer immediately told Chiune that there was no question in his mind about the foreign language that he should choose. It would be a choice that benefited him with the greatest advantages. He expounded upon Japan's current efforts towards exploration and development of Manchuria. Since Russia and Manchuria shared common borders for thousands of miles and also because Russia was well aware of the potential for development of Manchuria, both countries had great interest in developing its vast untapped resources. Both countries also realized the importance of being the first to gain important footholds into Manchuria. They both also appreciated Manchuria's strategic location in terms of defense and accessibility. Therefore, according to the friendly manager, there was no doubt in his mind that the Russian language would be the most important language that should be chosen under the prevailing conditions. Chiune was quick to grasp the validity of the assessments of this kindly manager. He realized how important communication with the Russians would eventually become and recognized that learning the Russian language would be a valuable asset to have as an officer of the Foreign Ministry. He thanked the kindly officer for his invaluable advice and left the office secure in the thought that his decision to learn Russian was a very good one.

Finally, in October of 1919, with feelings of great anticipation and optimism, Chiune arrived in Harbin. He was assigned to enter the special Russian language school at Harbin Gakuin for foreign ministry students. The founder of Harbin Gakuin was Shimpei Goto. He was an innovative thinker and he had originally developed a master plan for an efficient system of mass transportation for Tokyo. Unfortunately, it was never implemented during his lifetime due to budgetary deficits. However, due to his ideas, one of the finest examples of mass transportation exists in Tokyo today. Another side of Shimpei Goto is the fact that he was considered to be one of the great thinkers or theoreticians of his time. He advocated the idea that Japan's "manifest destiny," was the colonizing of under-developed countries such as China. By helping to provide educational advancements, technological development, and providing protection from advancing western encroachment, Japan would stop the spread of Communist ideology into Asia. Unfortunately, this brand of colonialism also encouraged strong military development and presence. However, for young Chiune, enrolling at Harbin Gakuin, only helped to further reinforce the philosophy of the importance of service to the people, a philosophy that he had embraced at Waseda University. Although Shimpei Goto did advocate for Japanese colonialism in the backward countries of Asia, he also stressed teaching about the importance of service to others as a most worthwhile goal to be achieved. Shimpei Goto set forth three doctrines that became the mottoes for Harbin Gakuin. The doctrines were the following: Service to others; not to serve for the sake of oneself; and not to expect rewards for services rendered. Quite interestingly, both of the institutions that Chiune attended strongly emphasized the importance of service and it appears to have greatly influenced him. Again, we come across the common threads or patterns that consistently appeared throughout in his life; in this instance, the emphasis on service to the people and community.

Living in Manchuria transformed his life. He was in a foreign place and experiencing an entirely different environment. His long held dream to travel and to learn about exotic places was now a reality. The primitive living conditions, the harsh climate, and the scarcity of modern conveniences did not affect his enthusiasm. Instead, it invigorated him because he loved the frontier atmosphere of a developing country. He loved the diversity in architecture and especially loved the onion shaped domes inspired by Russian designs. He enjoyed the cosmopolitan atmosphere, the diversity in people, food, smells and the sense of freedom. Harbin was a city burgeoning with activity and growth. He especially relished the cultural and ethnic diversity that existed there. Here was a city inhabited by ethnic Chinese, Koreans, Russians, Americans, Europeans, Jews, Japanese and many other peoples from different places that he had never known existed. There were many pockets or enclaves within the city, each with their distinctive sights, smells, sounds and exotic characteristics. He especially loved to visit the unique delicatessens, bakeries, and cafes in the Jewish section. He enjoyed the opportunity to speak in Russian to the Jewish inhabitants and to the White Russians who spoke that language. He savored his new life and appreciated the opportunity to live the life that he had always dreamed about as a child. At Harbin Gakuin, his brilliance quickly became apparent. His instructors recognized his superior ability to learn languages. His rapid acquisition and articulation in Russian was considered phenomenal. Everyone agreed that he spoke Russian almost like a native.

HIS GRIEF

"Every man can master a grief but he that has it."
Willliam Shakespeare

During the course of his education at Harbin Gakuin, his education was interrupted because he was drafted in the service of the "voluntary" Japanese army. It was 1920, and he was 20 years old. All eligible males were expected to serve for at least one year. He was assigned to the 79th Regiment, 9th Company. It was an outpost in Korea, in the far outreaches of that country. He knew that he would be uncomfortable in a military environment and disliked the pressures of living under authoritative conditions. He chose to regard this assignment as a short juncture in his life and as a part of his life experience. He also realized that his one-year service period would pass quickly. He was informed that due to his educational status, he was given the rank of Reserve Lieutenant. All was not so bleak because there was one ray of sunshine. It was the anticipation and hope that he would soon have the opportunity to visit his family and he eagerly anticipated for that day to come quickly. Since he was stationed in Korea, he was now closer to his mother and family who were still living there. As he patiently awaited the arrival of a pass that would give him time off, Chiune hoped for at least a couple of days to visit his family. He especially looked forward to visiting with his beloved mother whom he had not seen for a long time.

Tragedy struck on August 21, 1921. It was the most tragic day of his life. Up to this point in his life, he was a happy person and considered himself fortunate. But on this day in August while he was on field duty, he received the devastating message that his mother had passed away. After bearing six children, raising the children, keeping up the household as well as taking over the responsibilities of running the family business, she passed away, still a young woman who was still in her early forties. Chiune had always been keenly aware of the fact that she was physically frail and he had always worried about her health. He remembered how she tirelessly worked each day and late into the night. He lamented over the fact that his hopes to pay a surprise visit to his mother was not ever to be. He had been looking forward to the

(top) In uniform, Chiune Sugihara visits his family in Korea. It is believed that this photo was taken after his mother's funeral. (bottom) At age 20, he was drafted into the Japanese army. He was given the rank of Reserve Lieutenant. Chiune is in the second row, 2nd from the left.

visit and thought of it everyday. The delay in his planned visit was because he was on field duty. His grief became greater and he could not control his tears as he realized the he had missed meeting his beloved mother once more before she passed away. His feelings of loss, emptiness and great sadness was so profound that he expressed his feelings in his diary. He wrote that he could not control the tears of sadness that poured from his eyes. He wrote about his grief over the fact that did not have the chance to see her for at least one more time before she passed away. He remembered her kindness and the many hours they shared together as she told him stories of olden times and about how she hoped that he would grow up to be a person of compassion, with both inner and physical strength and compassion. It was she who had urged him to follow the path of Bushido.

Chiune had received the news of his mother's death during the afternoon while he was on field duty. As soon as he was relieved from his duty, he immediately went to his quarters to set up an altar for her. He described in his diary, his frantic efforts to prepare an altar for her by placing a photo and two candles in front of a makeshift stand. He indicated the time was approximately 4:30 in the late afternoon. As he looked upon his mother's photo, he could not take his eyes away from her image as he continued to experience great outpourings of grief. According to his diary, his emotional state was so great that he came to a state of unconsciousness and was not able to be aroused until about 4:00 AM. Upon his awakening, he noticed that three or four small candles had burnt out. He admonished himself for being careless and wasteful for not using one large candle instead of several small candles. Then he consoled himself for his lapse of common sense by thinking that the important thing was that he did light candles for his mother as soon as possible. Due to his severe emotional stress, he described how he experienced severe stomach pains. He wrote that as soon as it was possible, he went to a shop to purchase a proper altar (obutsudan). While out in the courtyard of the place where he went to buy the altar, he writes about an unusual experience that can be described as almost mystical. According to his writings, he tells about seeing some birds in the courtyard, but instead of hearing their usual chirping, he heard sounds of lamentation emitted from the birds. He wrote poetically that even the birds understood the depth of his sadness and were joining him in his grief.

Chiune was able to get permission to get time off in order to attend his mother's funeral service. A family photo taken after the funeral service shows that it was a lavish one with many huge wreathes of flowers surrounding the coffin and attended by many friends and relatives. Chiune is photographed dressed in military dress and is standing with a somber expression in front of a large banner with his mother's name on it. Chiune mentioned in his diary that after the funeral services, his three brothers accompanied him to the train station to see him off because he had to return to his post. He remained in the army until his tour of duty was completed. When he returned to Harbin, Manchuria, he was still unable to shake off sad memories about the loss of his dearly beloved mother.

PART III: DIPLOMATIC SERVICE (1924-1935)

THE FOREIGN MINISTRY (MANCHURIA)

"....But life is a great adventure, and the worsts of all fears is the fear of living."
Theodore Roosevelt

A few months after his return to Harbin, Chiune graduated from his school. He completed all of his required courses and graduated in 1924. He was happy to readjust to civilian life. Although he had just recently experienced profound grief, he was slowly able to again savor the delights of the city and to enjoy a sense of freedom that he missed during his army service. He vowed to set his army experience behind him and was determined to look forward to his future with renewed vigor and optimism. Very soon after graduation, he was appointed to be a clerk in the Japanese Foreign Embassy in the Russian section. He knew that as a diplomat trained through the exchange program, he would be limited in his promotions because he was not a graduate of the more prestigious universities such as Tokyo (Todai) University. It was commonly understood that unless one came from a prestigious family with a long history in diplomatic service or was a graduate of a top rated university, attainment of a high level position was very unlikely. Chiune accepted his status and happily undertook his new assignment with great enthusiasm. The fact is that he often found himself quite awed by his good fortune to be a part of the ministry and found it amazing that he was really working in Harbin for the foreign ministry. He often thought about when he was a young boy from a small rural village in Gifu Prefecture, dreaming of traveling and learning languages someday. On these occasions, he felt both happy and incredulous that it had all become a reality. He loved his country, Japan, and was proud to be a young man serving his country. Like many of his fellow student, he was caught up with the nationalistic fervor of those times and proud to serve his country well.

He found satisfaction in his job and also had an active social life with his colleagues. After working hours, he and his cohorts headed for the local popular dinner houses, bistros and cafes that had sprung up throughout Harbin. They all looked forward to an evening of relaxation, good food and any other amusing distractions that came their way. They were all young and looked forward to the casual atmosphere of the cafes and the camaraderie that they shared together. They enjoyed the music and liked watching the dancers while imbibing on the alcoholic beverages that flowed freely. They became acquainted with the waitresses, entertainers and the regulars who frequented the most popular cafes. Their visits to the café's became a regular part of their lives because they enjoyed the conviviality of café society.

Chiune was one of the most highly respected among his colleagues and they admired him for his unique talents and capabilities. However, they soon discovered that Chiune also stood out among them in another unique way. It was his unusual ability to drink great quantities of alcohol without any apparent visible effects. His friends were in awe of the fact that after a long night of singing and drinking, he seemed to be immune to all the normal symptoms associated with imbibing large quantities of alcohol. Unlike his companions, signs of any effects on him from drinking all night could not be detected. His strong constitution became legendary and this unusual trait was greatly admired by his companions. It just became one more thing that was admirable about Chiune. It was also reputed that when it came to drinking vodka, there was not a Russian that could outlast Chiune. Although the advisability of having such a characteristic can be considered to be a questionable one, it did prove to be a useful one later in his life.

HIS FIRST MARRIAGE

"You cannot pluck roses without fear of thorns, nor enjoy a fair wife without danger of horns."
Benjamin Franklin

On their frequent visits to the cafes and bistros, Chiune and his colleagues met and socialized with the local clientele. The core of his friends were his colleagues from the Japanese embassy, but they all enjoyed camaraderie with other customers that regularly frequented their favorite places. Harbin was a cosmopolitan city and there were opportunities to meet people of varied backgrounds and there were many young men who worked for embassies of different countries. Among the people that they often spent enjoyable evenings with were the white Russians. Chiune and his friends worked in the Russian section. They found it stimulating to converse and share stimulating stories in Russian. Many white Russians had escaped to Harbin during the time of the overthrow of the Romanov Dynasty, or more commonly known as the Bolshevik Revolution. It was a revolution in which the Proletarians overthrew the large landowners and the ruling class. When they took over, they demanded and instituted massive land reforms. Many of the Russians living in Harbin had been landowners or were connected to the ruling class. Belonging to this defunct upper class, most of them had lost everything and escaped with only their lives. It was estimated that about two million Russians were forced to flee Russia and to begin life anew. They were also considered to be stateless people. Chiune enjoyed great rapport with the white Russians especially because he liked conversing with them in Russian. In fact he even lived with a white Russian family for a short time in Harbin while he was still a student. It was common practice for the young recruits in the embassies to live in homes of sponsoring families because it was inexpensive and the people who provided them with room and board were able to earn a bit of income. It was a reciprocal situation for all the parties involved because it benefited each participant. For the students living in this kind of arrangement, it was also an opportunity to have more exposure to a foreign language, as it was for Chiune.

During their frequent social outings, it was not unusual for the Japanese men to meet and become friends with many of the Russian ladies who frequented the cafes. It was during one of these evenings that Chiune met Klaudia Semionova Apollonov, an attractive and vivacious young lady who was admired for her fine dancing. The fact is not substantiated, but many believe that she was one of the dancers at the café. The old cliché, that opposites attract, could be one of the reasons that they were drawn to each other. While Chiune tended to have a more introspective personality, Klaudia was outgoing and immensely popular among the café society. Apparently, Chiune was attracted to her fun loving nature and she soon won him over. It was common for his friends and colleagues to have friendly relations with women who were not Japanese, but most of them did not regard them as serious relationships. However, as usual, Chiune had a different attitude. He regarded all of his relationships sincerely and seriously and told his friends about his intention to ask her to marry him. His friends were dismayed by his announcement and cautioned him to delay his decision. Chiune believed that it was his own decision to make because it involved his personal feelings and he could not be moved to think otherwise.

Klaudia and Chiune were married in 1924. He was 24 and she was 21 years of age. It was said that she came from a family connected with Russian nobility. That fact was not unusual because many of the Russian refugees were in some manner connected to the Romanov family. She introduced him to a new kind of life that she loved and wanted to share with him. He became an aficionado of the ballet and classical music. They attended many of the ballet events and concerts that were performed in Harbin. He was introduced to the music of Beethoven and loved the Moonlight Sonata so much that he taught himself to play it on the piano. He also became an avid fan of the circus and loved attending the Russian circus for the rest of his life. He learned to love the spirited and melancholy Russian folk songs and liked to sing them at parties and gatherings. He wholeheartedly embraced and accepted this new culture and in many ways, he was more comfortable with his newly adopted culture and many aspects of his new life were much to his liking. Klaudia expanded Chiune's exposure to a world that he was not familiar with and he enjoyed and appreciated becoming more culturally developed and became a worldly sophisticate. He was grateful to Klaudia for introducing him to a life that he had not been exposed to before. Klaudia even encouraged him to accompany

Chiune Sugihara; photo taken circa 1924. He was now well on his way to rise among the ranks of the Manchurian Foreign Ministry.

her to the Russian Orthodox Church. He began to attend the services regularly and he became inspired by the sermons that he heard and became curious about Christianity. As he continued to attend services with Klaudia, he decided to learn more about Christianity. His closest exposure to organized religion had only been the family's observances of Shinto rites for special services. Shinto was not a religion, it was primarily ancestral worship and for observances of special services on ceremonial occasions such as weddings and funerals. His curiosity eventually led him to diligently study the Bible. As he began to understand the compassion and grace of the Bible's teachings, he made the decision to convert to Christianity. He was baptized and given a Christian name. His sense of spirituality that he was exposed to from his mother inspired him to embrace this religion because he loved the message of love, forgiveness and redemption.

As soon as he married Klaudia, he quickly discovered that he was also expected to care for her parents and other family members. As a result, he essentially supported Klaudia and her family. Becoming part of a Russian family, allowed for opportunities to become more familiar with some of their characteristics. He was intrigued with the great differences of his own culture and this newly adopted one because it was so unlike those of his family and his Japanese upbringing. He felt at ease with this new way of life and enjoyed the spontaneity, melancholy, and sense of humor that he observed and experienced. But he was also curious and felt disturbed when he sensed the animosity that his in-laws sometimes expressed about the Jews living in some parts of Harbin. However, Klaudia dismissed these sentiments because she apparently did not share those feelings. Because Chiune was not familiar with the Judeo-Christian traditions nor understood who or what it meant to be Jewish, he dismissed such behavior as a kind of misinformed and undesirable attitude. He did not ponder it seriously because his increasingly busy life kept him preoccupied with other concerns. Curiously, Chiune seemed to deeply appreciate the Russian dark sense of humor. Later in his life, he was inclined to share some of those Russian jokes that he remembered from his days in Harbin. His audience comprising of his Japanese friends or family just did not get it and wondered why Chiune thought his Russian jokes were so funny. As a result of becoming a part of a Russian family, he became even more articulate in the language and more than ever, spoke the language like a native Russian.

THE FOREIGN MINISTRY (MANCHUKUO)

"To give real service you must add something which cannot be bought or measured with money, and that is sincerity and integrity."
Donald A. Adams

Emperor Taisho passed away in 1926. It was the end of the Taisho Period and the beginning of one of the longest reigns in Japanese history with the ascension of Emperor Hirohito. His reign called the Showa Era lasted for 63 years. Chiune had by now several years of experience serving in the Foreign Ministry. During those years he was assigned to many different positions. As his responsibilities grew, his stature and reputation also grew and he rose within the ranks. His outstanding ability to translate Russian to Japanese or vice versa was common knowledge to all of his superiors. He was given the assignment to translate the most sensitive and important documents. One of his translation works from Russian to Japanese was a 600 page treatise titled, " A Report on the Economy of the Soviet Republic." It was such an outstanding piece of work that it became a landmark example of a work of translation for its conciseness and accuracy. He was acclaimed for his ability and recognized for his extraordinary competence. Since he was still supporting Klaudia and her extended family, he was burdened with many extra expenses. In 1929, he was offered a position as a part time instructor at Harbin Gakuin. Chiune accepted this offer not only because it would help to offset his mounting household expenses, but also because he enjoyed teaching. He taught classes in Russian grammar, reading and lectured on current events related to economics and politics. He remained in this teaching position for three years. During these years he took frequent trips back to Japan and visited his family who now lived in Nagoya. On many of these trips, Klaudia accompanied him and she became acquainted with his family. Apparently, the family had no problem accepting a non-Japanese person as part of the family. Chiune even gave her a Japanese name so she was sometimes called Yuriko, which meant Lily. She became especially close with Chiune's sister, Ryuko, the youngest and only girl in the family. Ryuko often went to visit Klaudia and Chiune in Manchuria. Ryuko and Klaudia got along very well and Ryuko enjoyed long visits with them. The relationship between Chiune and Klaudia appeared to be a good one and they seemed to get along very well. However, there was one problem, their relationship was marred by the fact that Chiune wanted to settle down to a more settled life while Klaudia wanted to continue her frenzied social one and did not want children. While Chiune hoped to have a family with many children, Klaudia did not want to change her life style. He realized that he had a serious dilemma and he hoped that Klaudia would have a change of heart and settle down soon.

By 1932, Manchuria became a puppet state of Japan and became known as Manchukuo. In March of that year, Chiune received a promotion to become Deputy Consul of the Manchurian Foreign Office. He was no longer working for the Japanese Foreign Ministry. Instead, he was serving in the Manchukuo Foreign Ministry that was essentially under a militaristic regime controlled by the Kwantung, the Japanese military force in Manchukuo. A great gap existed between the government in Tokyo and the military powers in Manchukuo. It was common for the Kwantung army to ignore orders from the Tokyo government. The Kwantung army's presence was justified under the guise that they provided the security and protection of Japanese territorial property and rights acquired as a result of the Russo-Japanese War of 1904. They were also supposedly there to insure the safety of the Japanese settlers who had recently emigrated there in massive numbers for the purpose of settlement and development. Japanese holdings such as the South Manchurian Railroad, the Liaotung Penninsula, Port Arthur, Darien, coal, forest and mining developments and other foreign investments needed to be protected. Following an eloquent appeal justifying Japan's move to create the independent state of Manchukuo in 1932,

Chiune seated next to Klaudia on a visit to Nagoya to visit his father and family. His father, Yoshimiza is standing next to Chiune's only sister, Ryuko.

by Yosuke Matsuoka, before the body of the League of Nations, the League voted against Matsuoka's appeal. Instead, they voted for autonomous rights in Manchuria under Chinese sovereignty. In retaliation, Japan seceded from the United Nations in 1933. Soon after that incident, Yosuke Matsuoka became Foreign Minister of Japan. It was under these political conditions and in a climate beset with criticism from the international community, that Chiune began his career with the Manchurian Foreign Ministry. Given Chiune's personal disdain about the military, it is very likely that he began his new career with a sense of uneasiness and some misgivings upon realizing that he was in reality working under a militaristic regime.

It was clearly evident to everyone that Chiune was becoming one of the fastest rising stars in the Manchurian ministry. Two months later, in May, he was given another special assignment to be an interpreter in the Russian section of the Manchurian Foreign Office. Within the same year, he was promoted again to become a Deputy Representative. Sometime during this period, a devastating natural disaster hit the area. It was a very disastrous situation that affected thousands of farmers and people in the villages. The flooding caused total destruction to all the farms, and in their crops and homes. In order to survive and to get resettled, the devastated victims needed supplies, food, clothing, medication, etc. There was a shortage of drinking water, doctors and places of shelter. They were in dire need of aid from the government and needed someone to provide guidance and to also provide leadership and direction because everything was in a state of confusion. The victims were Chinese and Korean farmers and they sought aid from the occupying government. As soon as Chiune was informed about their dire need for services, he immediately requested the formation of a task force to provide aid as soon as possible. His pleas fell on deaf ears and the attitude of his officers was that there were more immediate concerns that needed to be addressed. He clearly understood that the officials had no desire to get involved so he took it upon himself to go to the areas of devastation in order to assess the situation. He traveled to the remote back areas of the affected areas and saw with his own eyes the severity of the damage. The villagers were astounded to see the rare sight of an official from the front office willing to leave his desk job and to expose himself to the severe discomforts and severe lack of food and water to inspect and assess the devastation personally. They appreciated and admired his willingness to suffer all the discomforts caused by the disaster and to work with the locals under extremely severe weather conditions. He gave them advice and direction and taught them the techniques that he knew of that would help them to get back on their feet as soon as it was possible. It is not known how long he stayed to help, but those desperate farmers never forgot what Chiune had done for them. They were able to repay him at a later time for the care and kindness that he had extended to them. Why, how and what they did later was another miracle to come in the life of Chiune Sugihara.

His advancements continued to come in rapid succession. By June 28, 1933, he had been elevated to the position of Secretary General of the Northern Manchurian Railroad. This was a pivotal point in his career. As secretary general, he held the responsible position as the representative for the purchasing office for the purchase and development of the Manchurian Railroad. This assignment was indicative of the high respect and confidence that his superiors had for him. The purchase of the railroad was a key project because it was vitally significant for the eventual control and development of Manchukuo by Japan. Japan had already taken complete control over the Southern Manchurian Railroad on November 11, 1906, following their victory over Russia during the Russo Japanese War in 1904. Japan's ultimate plan was to take complete control of the Siberian railroad route. To have complete control of this important and strategic transportation system would secure an important foothold and insure Japan's power and presence in Manchukuo. A few years earlier when Chiune first began his diplomatic career, little did he dream that a farm boy from a rural area in Gifu Prefecture would be given the honor and responsibility of being an important part of Japan's growing global influence and dominance in Asia. Such a dream was unrealistic at a time when educational background and social standing were mandatory prerequisites for advancement. For Chiune, this reality was his personal miracle.

Taken during the Northern Manchurian Purchase negotiations. Chiune Sugihara is 6th from the left.

THE RAILROAD PURCHASE

"The struggle of life and death of an Empire"
Kozo Tamura, Japanese Industrialist

One of the chief problems facing Japan at this time was the state of Japanese-Soviet Union relations. The most important point of contention involved control over the Northern Manchurian Railroad. Due to their serious international economic problems, they suffered huge financial deficits in their economy. The Soviets finally decided to sell the railroad to Manchukuo. The railroad was built and managed jointly by China and the Soviet Union and the plan was to sell it to Manchukuo; however, essentially, it was to be purchased by Japan. Control of the railroad would insure control and security for approximately more than 1,600 million yen or about 70% of Japan's foreign investment and would be a primary factor in facilitating travel and development of the country.

Chiune fully appreciated the magnitude of the responsibility that was placed on him through his new position as secretary general for the purchasing department of the Northern Manchurian Railroad. Whether the fact that his superior, Chuichi Ohashi, chairman of the railroad project, was from Gifu Prefecture as was Chiune, could have influenced his being appointed to this position is pure speculation. However, their paths seemed to cross at different junctures in their careers. Chiune's job was to research and to put together the true market value of the railroad. The Soviets asking price was 250 million yen, an astounding figure when one compared it to Japan's national budget that was about two billion yen a year. The Kwantung army, who controlled Manchukuo was offering 50 million yen. Because of the huge difference between the asking price and the offering price, a deadlock or impasse in the negotiations existed. The success of the negotiations, therefore, hinged upon Chiune's ability to get an accurate assessment of the true value of the railroad. It is at this point in the story where one of the wonderful acts of fate again appeared in the life of Chiune Sugihara. In order to understand, it is necessary to now go back to the time when Chiune personally decided to help the victims of that disastrous flood. Those Chinese and Korean farmers who lived in the villages and backwoods of that area not only worked as farmers on their land, but during the off-season, most of them worked for the railroad companies. When they heard the news that the person who had once been their benefactor was in charge of getting accurate facts and figures for the true value of the railroad, they wanted to return the kindness that was given to them and volunteered to help him. What they essentially volunteered to do was to be his spies and obtain accurate information concerning labor and material expenses, revenues and receipts, profit and loss information, and all the other essential information needed to arrive at an accurate price for the true value of the railroad. Because they worked in different sections of the railroad, they were in a unique position to help him from various standpoints. Due to the help of his more than 100 "volunteers," he was able to come up with a very realistic figure as to the true market value of the railroad. As a result, due in large part to his findings, the railroad was bought at a much lower price and Japan was able to save millions of dollars.

Those negotiations began in the summer of 1933, and finally ended in March of 1935, when Yurenev, representative for the Soviet Union and Koki Hirota, Foreign Minister of Japan signed the final agreement for the purchase of the railroad. Chiune had spent about two years of his life working tirelessly day and night. Besides going out into the field to check out information, he attended at least 56 major meetings with top officials and was involved in countless smaller discussions. Under his superior, Ohashi, he met regularly with Japanese, Chinese, and Soviet representatives. Many of their meetings were covered in newspapers in Manchukuo, China, Japan and the Soviet Union because it was one of the leading official projects of that time. There is great suspicion that one of the leading Soviet delegates named Kazarovsky, never forgot about Chiune Sugihara and the contribution that he made in coming up with the final price for the railroad because there is reason to believe that he later played a role in determining Chiune's future.

HIS MENTOR, HIROTA, KOKI

"Associate yourself with men of good quality if you value your reputation, for it is better to be alone than in bad company."
George Washington

Koki Hirota, will be referred to as Hirota, Koki for this part of the story because Chiune referred to him in the Japanese style of identifying the family name first, followed by the given name. It is believed that by learning about Hirota, Koki, it will open the door towards a better understanding of Chiune Sugihara because Chiune was never one to expose his personal thoughts and beliefs. He never discussed his politics or opinions openly with anyone. He was a very private person and preferred to listen to others and absorbed what he read and heard like a sponge. Because of his tendency to keep everything private, he was described as being enigmatic. People also had a tendency to describe him as elusive and eccentric. These kinds of descriptive words lent to creating a persona for Chiune as someone involved in intrigue and secretiveness. It further enhanced the notions and speculations that he might indeed have been a spy or even a double agent. His job as a vice consul or a member of a Legation did involve doing intelligence work. However, there is no real evidence that he was really a "spy." Fortunately, for those who desire to get a closer glimpse into the true nature of Chiune, he did leave a clue about what he believed in. That clue was the fact that he showed his admiration for Hirota, Koki, by naming his first born son after him. Naming his son was an important decision for Chiune. He was not the kind of person to make an important decision without putting in a lot of thought and care before making up his mind. Therefore, the fact that he did choose to name his son after him gives us a strong clue.

Hirota, Koki was found guilty on all counts as a war criminal by the Tokyo Tribunal on War Crimes, and executed by hanging on December 28, 1948. This man is the very person that Chiune Sugihara considered as his mentor and role model. Many people would question why and how could anyone come up with this conclusion about a man who had a very strong tendency to be private and to keep his thoughts to himself. The answer is that he simply told his eldest son, Hiroki, that he was named after Hirota, Koki because he was the one person that he most admired and considered as his role model about being a decent human being. He also explained to Hiroki that although their names were not similar in sound, both names were written in the same Japanese character. He advised Hiroki to someday find out why he was named after him. Hiroki regarded this revelation as most telling and regarded it as a key to understanding his father's true character. After many years of reading about this man that he was named after, Hiroki believed that he eventually came to better understand about the kind of person his father was and he was proud to bear the name given to him. This small detour from the story of Chiune is believed to be appropriate and necessary because it is believed that understanding a little about Hirota, Koki will be quite helpful towards understanding Chiune. It is also at this point in the story of Chiune Sugihara, that we come upon the many opportunities that he had to have been in direct or indirect contact with Koki, in order to develop the admiration that he had for him.

In order to learn a bit more about the person Chiune most admired, it would be helpful to learn something about Hirota, Koki's background. He was born in Fukuoka Prefecture on Kyushu Island on February 28, 1878 to the family of a humble stonemason. He was given the simple name, Jotaro, which meant strong and sturdy person. However, like many Japanese, he believed that one's name identified his character so he painstakingly took it upon himself to go through all the legal maneuvers and officially changed his name to Koki. Koki meant broadminded and firm of purpose. It was this name written with the same Japanese calligraphy that Chiune chose to give to his first born son, Hiroki. Koki, like Chiune was born in the backwoods of Japan and was quickly recognized for being extremely intelligent and talented in many areas such as martial arts, literature and especially calligraphy. The townspeople and leaders of the community quickly recognized his high academic abilities and provided a scholarship fund to cover his expenses to continue his education at a prestigious university. They felt that they did not want a student with his great potential to become a stonemason like his father; although his father was highly respected and admired by the townspeople. They believed that his talents should not be wasted and that he would someday bring pride to his community with his great accomplishments. It is truly a heartwarming story about the people of his town. Hirota, Koki always remained a humble country boy at heart and never forgot his roots. Like Chiune, he too excelled academically and was admired by many for his accomplishments. The difference between Chiune and Koki is that Koki did eventually graduate from Tokyo University. As a result, despite his humble beginnings, he became a career diplomat. Whereas, Chiune, having graduated from an exchange type university program instead of a prestigious university, could never be considered to become a high level career diplomat.

Hirota, Koki's first important appointment as a career diplomat was as minister to Holland who headed that Legation. After serving in different posts in different country's such as England, China, Korea, Soviet Union, etc., he was selected to be the Foreign Minister of Japan from 1933 to 1936. Those years, from 1933-1936, was when the negotiations for the Northern Manchurian Railroad took place and Hirota, Koki was Foreign Minister of Japan. Thus, Chiune must have had many opportunities to have some form of communication with Koki due to the fact that Koki was head of the project and eventually signed the purchase agreement with the Soviets in 1935. It should also be remembered that there were over 50 high level meetings during those negotiations when Chiune had opportunities to meet Koki. In 1936, soon after the conclusion of the railroad purchase, Hirota, Koki was installed as Prime Minister of Japan on March of 1936. During his office as Prime Minister, the Nanking Massacre occurred. The Kwantung army was completely out of control from the Tokyo government. Hirota vehemently chastised the conduct of the army as completely scandalous and incomprehensible. He was caught up in the midst of the tidal wave toward militaristic fervor and did not have the authority or power to quell it. As Prime Minister, he had always consistently advocated for peaceful and diplomatic solutions to any kind of discord that his country faced. However, the outrageous and irresponsible actions of the army made him culpable and a party to those events in Nanking. To the eyes of the rest of the world, who did not understand Japanese politics, he was immediately regarded as the responsible party because the fact remained that he was indeed the Prime Minister of Japan when it occurred. After that massacre, popularly known as "Rape of Nanking," he resigned as Prime Minister. Despite the fact that it was because of the army's irresponsible actions that the massacre occurred, he took full responsibility for what happened during his office. His reasoning was that as Japan's Prime Minister, he failed in his responsibility by failing to prevent the massacre and was therefore, the responsible party. As mentioned previously, although he realistically did not have the power or authority to curtail the army's actions, he truly believed that as leader of his country when the tragedy occurred, he had failed his people and country. After the defeat of Japan, during the Tokyo Tribunal for war criminals, he was accused of war crimes due to the Nanking Massacre. During the trials, he did not cooperate fully with his defense team towards proving his innocence. Instead, he accepted the guilty verdict given out by the Tokyo Tribunal and thereby accepted full responsibility for what happened at that time. One of the judges sitting on the trial named V. A. Roling, a judge representing the Netherlands, was the only dissenting judge and voted for his acquittal. Judge Roling believed that as a civilian Prime Minister under the provisos of the Japanese government, Koki was powerless to change the actions of the army; therefore, not guilty of war crimes. Hirota, Koki was the only civilian leader that was executed as a result of the trials. The others sentenced to death and guilty of war crimes were found culpable because of their military activities. Throughout the trials, observers noticed and admired Hirota, Koki's stoic demeanor and consistent dignity. He was once quoted as saying, "A diplomat does not make excuses for his actions. It is up to posterity to judge his actions." He was also known for believing that a real statesman should not work in the limelight, rather should instead do the work that no one speaks of. Hirota believed that Japan's priority was to gradually build up international trust and to focus on diplomatic relations in order to avert aggression of any kind. Instead of making demands on territorial rights and interests, he believed his government should work on policies that created mutual trust and friendship. He discouraged any actions connected with extra-territoriality. He did not advocate for militarism, but he did believe in building a defense force for purposes of creating an effective deterrent against any colonialist encroachments. Hirota, Koki also never forgot his humble roots and only considered himself as a servant for his country and regarded receiving honors and accolades as hindrances to performing his tasks at hand. Chiune must have discerned the genuineness of how Hirota, Koki regarded himself and his dedication to serving his country well. Chiune's later actions showed how much he admired and embraced Koki's words illustrated by his deeds. Hiroki, his eldest son named after Hirota, Koki, always believed that his father hoped to be able to follow in the courageous giant steps of Hirota, Koki. Hiroki believed that his decision to name him after this man, was a true testimony of his regard for him.

Chiune's had many opportunities to meet him during the endless meetings that usually lasted for days during the railroad negotiations. For example, there was reported in the newspaper, The Tokyo Asahi Shimbun, dated September 23,1933, about talks concerning the Northern Manchurian Railroad (Hokutetsu). It announced that the meeting was to be held at the official residence of the Deputy Foreign Minister. It also listed the names of those attending the meetings as Messrs. Ohashi, Morikita, Sugihara, Iyo, Toriuchi, Kazarovsky, Kutznetov, Barischnikof, and Roszinski. Although Hirota, Koki's name does not appear on the list, it is not unreasonable to believe that he attended those meetings, however briefly, to provide his input and guidance. It is also well known and documented that Hirota, Koki actively took part in the negotiations at every stage of the project which lends further credence to the fact that Chiune had many opportunities to meet Hirota, Koki. Those meetings were not the only possible chances that Chiune had to get to know Koki well. It is suspected that Chiune may have been one of the many young career diplomats and young novices entering the foreign ministry to have visited Hirota, Koki at his private residence in Kugenuma, a small coastal town about 50 miles from Tokyo. It was a small seaside retreat near Fujisawa City that he had purchased in 1932. It was sheltered among pine trees and it was known as a place where many guests were openly welcomed. Koki was amenable to informal discussions and was always a good listener interested to hear what others were thinking about. The Sugihara Family always wondered why their father, Chiune, who came from the mountainous backwaters of Gifu was aware of this beautiful locale and made the decision to buy land there in order to build their first home. Hiroki, Koki's namesake always suspected that his father came to love that area because of going there to visit Koki and attending the many informal discussions held in Kugenuma. Whatever the relationship was between Chiune and Koki, they both exemplified in their conduct and integrity, a true dedication to try their best to serve their country and its people well.

ENDINGS AND NEW BEGINNINGS

"When two who love are parted, They talk, as friend to friend, clasp hands and weep a little, And sigh without an end."

Heinrich Heine

During the period in which Chiune was involved with negotiations for the railroad, he began to realize that his marriage to Klaudia was not improving nor going well. Their differences concerning the desire for children and family life could

Celebrating the negotiations of the Manchurian Railroad; March 1935.

no longer be ignored. In 1934, while still involved with the railroad negotiations, Chiune divorced Klaudia. They had been married for ten years. His sister Ryuko and a few of his colleagues were disappointed. Despite the divorce, they retained an amicable relationship and Chiune was generous in their divorce settlement. He gave Klaudia their house and apparently sent her funds and gifts for the rest of his life. It was believed that Klaudia immigrated to Australia and passed away in 1993.

Chiune continued to rise within the ranks of the Manchurian Foreign Ministry after the completion of the railroad negotiations. During this period, he had many opportunities to go to Tokyo on official visits. In 1934, the increased presence of the Manchurian forces, the Kwantung Army, was daily becoming more oppressive. It was clearly becoming evident that military presence was becoming a dominant force in Manchuria. Chiune had never been comfortable about being under military influence. He remembered the feelings of repression that he had experienced during his brief stint in the army. The army's presence was also affecting the general population. There were daily reports of acts of brutality upon the civilian citizenry. He himself witnessed acts of disrespect and even outright inhumane acts. He began experiencing a sense of deep shame that there were men in the Japanese army that behaved in those despicable ways. Due to the increasing sense of oppression that he felt with the ever-growing presence of the army, it became difficult for him to function effectively. He repeatedly sent in complaints and reports describing the terrible treatment by the soldiers upon the civilian population. Ethnically, most of these people were Chinese and Koreans. All of his grievances fell upon deaf ears. Despite his many complaints and reports to the authorities, he ironically received a generous offer from the army. It was an offer providing for a large budget that would enable him to organize an intelligence unit in the army. He was highly recommended because he was quite renowned for his linguistic abilities and for his organizational capabilities. No matter, he himself realized that he could no longer tolerate working under the repressive atmosphere that he experienced daily. He finally made the decision that it would be best for him to resign from the Manchukuo regime. Along with his signed resignation, he sent a letter of protest concerning the repressive treatment that the civilian population had to endure due to the inhumane behavior of the army. He not only sent in his resignation, but also included a formal letter of protest. When his superiors received his letter of resignation, they viewed his actions as incomprehensible. They could not understand how the person that was on the verge of receiving another promotion to become the Minister of Foreign Affairs for the Manchurian Foreign Ministry, could possibly jeopardize his career as a diplomat. They admonished him for his decision, reminding him about how he was compromising his career, and implored him to seriously reconsider his decision to resign. Following his usual pattern of behavior, Chiune stood by his decision and returned to Tokyo. Once again he had made the decision to defy authority and to follow the dictates of his conscience. He believed that he was doing what was best under the prevailing circumstances and took heart in believing that his mother would have also approved. However, he left his post in Manchukuo with a sense of foreboding and hoped that the escalating presence of the army would soon abate.

Soon after his return to Tokyo, he happened to go shopping to buy a new tie at the Takashimaya Department Store. Working in the men's tie department, was an attractive young lady who offered to help him select his new tie. There was an immediate mutual attraction between them, and he stalled about his decision to buy the tie. After deciding to buy the tie, he asked that she keep the tie for him until he returned the next day when he would pick it up. He returned to the store some time later, and they struck up a friendly conversation and became acquainted with each other. The young lady working at the department store was Yukiko Kikuchi, who had recently moved to Tokyo. She was currently sharing an apartment with her brother, Shizuo, who was then working for the Nippon Life Insurance Company. Yukiko had moved to Tokyo from Shikoku Island. Her family life was unusual in that both of her parents were progressives. They were quick to adapt to the new Western ideas and styles and encouraged their children to be independent. Her father was the principal of a business high school and he introduced innovative ideas for the school. Her mother quickly acquired a taste for western fashion and was the first woman in the area to wear high heeled shoes and

Yukiko Sugihara met Chiune in Tokyo in 1935. They were married soon after in 1936.

western style dresses. Chiune enjoyed listening to Yukiko's ideas about her ambitions and about her artistic interests. Yukiko also found her new acquaintance to be an attractive and interesting person with some very unique characteristics. She enjoyed his sincerity and appreciated his thoughtful demeanor. Unlike so many Japanese men she had known in the past, he had a kind and gentle nature and was always willing to listen to her and was genuinely interested in her thoughts and opinions. They continued their friendship and began meeting quite frequently. Chiune became a regular guest at the apartment and also became a close friend to her brother Shizuo.

Pictured on the far left are Yukiko and Chiune attending a picnic with friends and colleagues soon after their wedding.

During their very brief courtship, Yukiko was puzzled over the fact that most of their outings involved visits to parks and other public facilities that did not require admission. They rarely went out to eat and he appeared to be very frugal. Yukiko realized that Chiune had a well paying position, so she decided to bring the matter up for discussion. He was very flustered and embarrassed to be confronted with this inquiry. He then explained to her his dilemma and why he was caught up in the current situation. He explained that he was in the midst of completing the necessary papers for getting a divorce and was making the payments in order to resolve all the legalities that entailed going through a divorce. Yukiko was very sympathetic about his current circumstances so they continued their frequent walks to the park and picnics along the lakes and rivers around Tokyo. Yukiko was fascinated to listen to Chiune tell about his experiences in Manchuria concerning the purchase of the Manchurian railroad. She sympathized with him as he told her about his resignation and admired him for his reasons to resign. In February of 1935, after a brief courtship, they were married in a very simple ceremony at the Greek Orthodox Church in Tokyo. Chiune still kept his Christian faith and Yukiko agreed to be baptized and was given the Christian name, Maria. She was 21 years of age, thirteen years younger than Chiune. He had convinced her that her interests and personality would fit well with his profession and that she would be a great asset to his career as well as a loving companion. But most importantly, she was in agreement with him about the importance of having children and a good family life. After their marriage, they settled in a section of Tokyo called Ikebukuro. There she met some of Chiune's Russian speaking colleagues and was fascinated by her new life with Chiune. In Yukiko's memoir, her description of their first meeting differed from the above because at that time, she felt that it might make her appear to be too forward for people of her generation. Today, the story of their first meeting would be appreciated and regarded as a very romantic one.

In December of 1935, Chiune was given notice that he was assigned to a post as an interpreter in the Moscow Japanese Embassy in the Soviet Union. Receiving this new assignment was in keeping with the usual changes and consistent with his background and his linguistic abilities. To the great surprise and consternation of the Japanese Ministry, they received denial for confirmation of Chiune's new appointment. This was cause for a big stir within foreign ministry circles because they had never been confronted with such an unexpected denial. The event even made headlines in all the newspapers. The Ministry sent out inquiries to the Moscow office seeking answers to this turn of events. They wanted to know why they considered Chiune Sugihara to be "persona non grata" in the Soviet Union. They never received a satisfactory reply. Chiune was of course greatly disappointed by this turn of events because his wildest dream was to someday become the Japanese Ambassador to Russia. If he were accepted for this appointment, it could have brought him closer to his dream. A curious reporter began his own personal investigation into the matter. His findings could not be substantially corroborated. However, he was able to discover that Kazarovsky, who had been the leader of the Soviet delegation during the railroad negotiations had recently become an influential member of the personnel department in Moscow. Could he still be holding a grudge against Sugihara for exposing the Soviet's attempt to sell the railroad far above its fair market value? Did he have something to do with denial of Chiune's new assignment? If that were indeed the fact, little did Kazarovsky realize that by denying Chiune that position in Moscow, he was inadvertently and indirectly responsible for Chiune Sugihara's eventual "Mission of Mercy" in Lithuania. A year after his marriage, an event of particular note happened on February of 1936. This incident became known as the 2.26 Incident because it happened on February 26. On that day, Tokyo was blanketed by the severest snowstorm not experienced since 1905. Yukiko, remembered that day quite clearly because Chiune received a call on that day and appeared to be quite perturbed after receiving his message. He immediately rushed out their home to his office. Yukiko repeatedly tried to call him all day to find out what had happened. She remembered that she had no word from him all that day and into the next day. He finally returned the following day and was reluctant to say too much about what had happened. She remembers the frustrations and anxieties that she experienced on that day waiting to hear from him. What actually occurred on that snowy day was an attempted coup de'tat by some 1400 young radical officers that represented the "Imperial Way." During the incident, many of the government leaders were killed and the then current Prime

Chiune is standing on the far left. He was a delegate in 1936 representing the Japanese Ministry to discuss fishing rights on the Sakhalin Islands with the Soviets.

Minister, Okada narrowly escaped with his life. The young radicals were from a very poor district in which many of the soldiers in the army were recruited. They were seeking drastic reforms to remedy the poor economic and social conditions prevalent among the farmers in the Northern Honshu district. Their cause was for the overthrow of the corrupt officials and reconstruction of a government free of economic and political corruption. The uprising mandated the imposition of martial law. Martial law was something that Chiune disliked because it involved military control. The mutineers surrendered about a week later and under this grim atmosphere, Hirota, Koki was sworn in as the new Prime Minister of Japan on March 3,1936. Again, Chiune could not shake off the sense of foreboding connected with escalation of a war-like atmosphere that he sensed was increasing in Japan. He remembered his many misgivings about the growth of military activity in Manchukuo when he left that country after handing in his resignation. Fortunately, at just about this time, there was also good news that helped to dispel many of Chiune's apprehensions. It was Yukiko's joyous news that Chiune was soon to become a father.

Chiune's next major assignment in 1936, was as a delegate to represent the Japanese Ministry to Kamchatka on the Sakhalin Islands. His assignment was to negotiate with the Soviets over fishing rights; especially for salmon in the fisheries of that region. Disagreements about fishing rights between the Soviets and the Japanese had been occurring with predictable regularity. These occurrences flared up from time to time since the Treaty of Portsmouth was concluded after the Russo-Japanese War of 1904. Disputes concerning fishing rights arose more frequently as fishing along coastal waters expanded. Finally when the Hirota-Karakhan Agreement, an agreement between the Soviet Union and Japan, was signed, limits were set as to the extent of territorial waters and the rights of each of the countries involved. Despite that agreement, disputes continued to arise regularly and Chiune's assignment was to act as a mediator to help bring about an agreeable compromise solution. Here again is another possible Chiune/Koki connection in the fact that Hirota, Koki was instrumental in completing the treaty involving fishing rights and that later, Chiune was given the assignment to represent Japan in helping to resolve disagreements connected with the Hirota-Karakhan agreement.

FATHERHOOD

"There is no friendship, no love, like that of the parents for the child."
Henry Ward Beecher

Chiune's long held wish to be a father was fulfilled when Yukiko gave birth to their first son on September 20, 1936. Unfortunately, when his new son was born, Chiune was on that assignment in Kamchatka involving the fishing agreements. But as soon as it was possible, he hurried back to Tokyo. Yukiko remembered that as Chiune held up his new baby, he exclaimed, "Look at me, I am your father." As stated earlier, Chiune proudly named his newborn son, Hiroki, in honor of the man that he considered to be his role model, Hirota, Koki. He enjoyed fatherhood and would be frequently seen rushing home from work in order to play with his new son. Everyone remembered him as a good father and his sons all agreed that he never spoke harshly nor never raised his hands to them. People who lived in their neighborhood commented on how young Hiroki favored his father in appearance and even strangers were prone to comment on their close resemblance. Hiroki was also baptized at the Greek Orthodox Church and was christened as Jacob.

Soon after Hiroki was born, Yukiko and Chiune were making preparations to get ready to move to his newly assigned post in Turkey. Just before their departure, they were informed that instead of going to Turkey, they would instead be going to Finland. This change was most probably due to the army's interest in getting information about activities in northern and eastern European countries because there were talks currently in progress about a possible alliance with Germany. Finland's proximity to Germany would be strategically more useful under the then existing current situation. The legation that he was assigned to was in Helsinki. Helsinki was considered to be a minor, backwater post. Chiune's job was to be the translator for the Japanese Legation there.

PART IV: EASTERN EUROPEAN ODYSSEY (1936-1946)

HELSINKI

Due to the change of plans, preparations had to be made to travel to Helsinki, Finland. Going to Finland, posed some new complications, because as you may remember, Chiune was regarded as persona non grata in the Soviet Union. As a result, it became necessary to travel to Finland via the United States rather than the usual route through the Soviet Union. Fortunately for the family, Yukiko's younger sister, Setsuko, had decided to travel with them. She wanted the experience of traveling abroad and was willing to help by being a nanny for young Hiroki. The necessity for taking a longer route caused several inconveniences that were mainly connected with traveling with an infant. The increased duration of travel time and other problems related to making connections in different places made the journey an arduous one.

Enroute to Finland on the ship, The Bremen. Chiune is pictured carrying young Hiroki, who acquired the name, Puppe, while on board the ship by the German passengers.

(top) A photo of a street in Helsinki circa 1936. (bottom) A family portrait taken during his assignment in Helsinki, 1938.

However, for Chiune, it was a wonderful opportunity to at last see the United States. This was the country that he had always wished to visit and his wish had come true. It turned out to be one of the most memorable experiences of his lifetime. After landing on the West Coast at Seattle, Washington, they traveled by train across the broad expanse of the United States. They went over the Rocky Mountains, across the Great Plains, and passed by the great mid-western cities. He was reminded about Siberia and Manchukuo as he traveled across the vast expanse of the United States continent and was impressed by the many large buildings and skyscrapers that he saw while passing through Chicago. Because their itinerary did not account for time changes within the United States, they barely made it on time to board their ship. Upon their arrival to New York, they hurriedly boarded their ship, The Bremen. From there, they crossed the Great Atlantic and finally disembarked upon the shores of Germany before heading to Finland. Crossing the Atlantic gave them the opportunity to wind down and they enjoyed the leisure activities aboard ship. There was one thing of note that did happen while crossing the Atlantic. Being the devoted father that he was, it became a daily habit for Chiune to carry his infant son out on deck each day to allow him to get fresh air and sunshine. Most of the guests on the Bremen were German and they became familiar with Chiune carrying his young son during their daily walks. By now Chiune had learned the rudiments of speaking in German and enjoyed engaging in friendly chats with the Germans on board. Instead of calling Hiroki by his name, the German guests preferred to address him as Puppe, which meant little doll. Yukiko and her sister, Setsuko also liked the sound of that name and they gradually began to call him Puppe instead of Hiroki.

Upon reaching the European shores of Germany, the Sugiharas, passed through Holland and Switzerland before reaching Finland. Finland was a country known as the land of many lakes. Minister Sako who headed the Helsinki Legation graciously welcomed them. Soon after preliminary introductions were made, Minister Sako immediately invited the family to live with him at his official residence. Because the Minister's wife and family were not living in Helsinki with him, he asked that Yukiko and Chiune help host the social functions given by the Japanese Legation. He also asked Yukiko to accompany him to any official function that he was required to attend. It became apparent that attending and hosting social parties and dances was at the top of the list of activities that took most of their time. There were round after round of social functions that they were required to attend regularly. They began to really appreciate Setsuko's help and presence and were grateful that she had decided to accompany them to Europe. They quickly realized that without her help, it would have been almost impossible to keep up with the round of activities and parties that they were expected to attend. One social event that remains vivid in Mrs. Sugihara's memory is that of attending a special dinner hosted by the renowned Finnish composer and conductor, Sibelius, who became well known for his composition, Finlandia. On this special occasion, he presented Yukiko with a signed photograph of himself that she treasured highly. Yukiko enjoyed the whirlwind of social activities and it suited her well. Chiune just tolerated it and regarded it as a part of his job.

Except for their socially active life, it was quiet in Helsinki and there were no obvious signs of the impending chaos that would soon reverberate all over Europe. For the Sugihara family, they enjoyed a bucolic life that consisted primarily of those never ending social functions. They also enjoyed their rare opportunities to go on special retreats to a cottage in the country during the summer. In late fall, their second child, another boy, was born to them on October 29, 1938. Anticipating and hoping that it would be a girl this time, Yukiko had already chosen the name Chiaki. Chiaki happened to be a Japanese name that was appropriate for either a boy or a girl, so Chiune and Yukiko kept the name Chiaki for their second son.

While the family was enjoying and getting accustomed to having another baby in the family, acceleration of military activity by Germans and Italians was increasing. Many people living in the western and central parts of Europe were becoming frightfully aware that they were living in unpredictable times. Due to advancing German forces, they were experiencing greater pressures and uncertainties about their future. By early March of 1938, Nazi forces had occupied Austria and decrees for mandatory registration of Jews were enforced. The Jewish problem was getting world attention and in April of that year, the Evian Conference was held to discuss the "Jewish Problems." Following trends instituted by Germany, Italy followed suit by enacting anti-Semitic laws. By October of 1938, the signing of the Berlin-Rome Axis pact between Germany and Italy confirmed their alliance. Following the occupation of Austria, western Czechoslovakia was next taken over. The letter "J" was required on all Jewish passports in order to discourage immigration, while over 17,000 Jewish Poles were expelled from Germany. In Germany, a pogrom called Kristallnacht (Night of the Broken Glass), occurred on a cold November night. On that night, hundreds of synagogues were destroyed and Jewish businesses were looted and destroyed while thousands of Jewish men were captured and sent to concentration camps. The sense of foreboding that Chiune had experienced when martial law was enacted in Japan, and again when he was in Manchukuo, where he observed the continuous escalation of military presence, was now being felt by him again as he received grim reports daily. Those reports of increasing turmoil were coming in quite frequently. While most of Europe was undergoing great unrest, life in Helsinki appeared to be relatively untouched by it all. However, there did exist an air of personal uncertainty about what Chiune's next assignment was going to be. For a while there was word that Japanese Ambassador Sugimura of France was requesting that Chiune be transferred to France for some intelligence work. However, Prime Minister Hirota, Koki overruled this request. The Prime Minister seemed to have the opinion that Chiune's linguistic talents would be of better use for other helpful purposes. Instead, he recommended re-assignment to Turkey where he had been assigned earlier before going to Finland; here again, another Koki-Chiune connection turns up. As Chiune anxiously waited to hear about what his next assignment might be, uncertainty and confusion were also growing stronger each day throughout Europe.

Despite the relatively quiet existence that prevailed in Helsinki, Chiune was acutely aware of what was happening outside of Helsinki. He had been reading letters and other messages concerning Nazi Germany's acts of rampant aggression, the chaotic atmosphere that permeated most of Europe, and reports about the Jewish problems. He clearly realized that the outlook for the future did not bode well. He was also aware that both Japan and Germany were having discussions about signing a pact. Talks of a stronger alliance with Germany was due to the strong influence of former army attache', Hiroshi Oshima, who was known to be fanatically pro-German. This attache' had just recently been appointed to be the Japanese Ambassador to Berlin. Chiune, who was pro-Western, was disturbed about these recent trends and sensed that there would be drastic changes in Japan's policies. Another fact that disturbed him at this time was that communications that he was receiving had begun to be more frequent. Even in a Legation considered to be an outpost, there was now an increase in daily communications.

Yukiko recalls in her memoir about Helsinki, the frequent visits to the Legation by persons notoriously known to be intelligence agents and operatives. Chiune was fully aware that during times of uncertainty and especially when there were talks about the formation of new alliances, the legations and consulates would be called upon to increase their surveillance and intelligence activities. Chiune disliked the idea of being a spy. Earlier in his career, while serving in Manchukuo, he was asked by the army to organize and to head an intelligence unit. He had refused and stated that he would never accept a position where it would be necessary for him to be incognito. He declared that the only positions that he would consider were those in which he would be able to make a decision and sign his name to that decision. Ironically, although the differences were subtle, Chiune seemed to differentiate between making surveillance reports as opposed to being an actual spy. He deemed that it was acceptable for him to issue detailed reports about his surveillance and observations activities because he considered it to be a part of his job to provide information needed by his country. He believed that it was his job to help his country to make good decisions based on reports received from the field. Therefore, he regarded those tasks as making intelligence reports and not "cloak and dagger" spying.

At the onset of 1939, German military activity increased to a much greater degree and their drive to take over Europe was now clearly evident. There was also great escalation of anti-Semitic activities. Hitler made a speech referring to Vernichtung (extermination) of Jews. By May of 1939, Germany had occupied Czechoslovakia. Then that was quickly followed by annexation of Bohemia and Moravia. The Molotov-Ribbentrop Pact, a non-aggression pact signed by Germany and the Soviet Union, was finalized by the end of August. Invasion of Poland by Germany marked the official beginning of WWII. The Germans had begun their rampage over Europe and the Third Reich appeared to be unstoppable. Polish Jews living in German occupied Poland were forced to wear armbands with yellow stars on them for purposes of identifying them as Jews.

Back in Asia, a continent away, the situation there was also getting out of control. Japan's army was running out of control in China. His mentor, Hirota, Koki, had recently become Prime Minister of Japan. He was faced with numerous challenges towards restoring order and to ameliorate the great damage the army had inflicted upon the reputation of Japan. The wanton behavior of the army in Nanking created critical worldwide reaction. These reactions were detrimental towards Koki's efforts to conduct any serious discussions with the United States or any other country. Worldwide reactions seriously jeopardized Japan's international relations with other countries. The Prime Minister was beset by numerous problems and sought solutions to rectify Japan's reputation. Along with all of these problems, Japan also faced threats of boycotts and the placing of embargoes on vitally needed supplies by the United States. On the European front, former army attache' and pro-German Japanese Ambassador Oshima, was in Berlin. He was intent upon strengthening his plans to create a Japan-Germany alliance. His success would profoundly affect Chiune's future.

As mentioned previously, even at the quiet Helsinki Legation, signs of unrest were increasing. In the midst of all of these catastrophic occurrences going on throughout Europe, the relatively peaceful existence of the Sugihara family was to change very soon. All speculations about what Chiune's next assignment might be suddenly came to a halt. An unexpected order was issued to Chiune from Tokyo from the Foreign Ministry. His new orders stated that he had been assigned to become the new Vice Consul of Lithuania. It was highly suspected that Japanese Ambassador Oshima of Berlin was influential in this sudden change. He was also informed that his appointment as Vice Consul was due to the fact that there were certain formalities that could be by-passed by his appointment as Vice Consul rather than that of Consul General. The assumption was that in order to speed up the new orders, it was for all intents and purposes, in the best interest to appoint him as Vice Consul. As the new Vice Consul, his job was to open up a small Consulate in the town of Kaunas, the capital of Lithuania. There had previously never been a Japanese Consulate in Lithuania. Why did they suddenly decide to establish one and why was Chiune appointed to that particular post?

NEW CHALLENGES

"We would accomplish many more things if we did not think them as impossible."
Christian G.Malensherbes

All of the previous events that occurred in Chiune's life, now seemed to be coming together towards fulfilling his destiny. It was becoming more apparent that he would be the person who would be at the right place at the right time. The right place, in this case, was Kaunas, Lithuania and the right time was July of 1940. In her memoir, Yukiko recalled that Kaunas was a very special sojourn in the family's European odyssey. The family had increased to a family with three boys and she

A family portrait taken in Kaunas, 1940, right after Haruki was born.

had memories of a happy family life there. She recalled the idyllic summer days that her children enjoyed while playing with the neighborhood children. She remembered feeling pleased as she listened to Hiroki, her eldest son, speaking in fluent German. They were very comfortable and enjoyed living there. Unlike life in Helsinki, their social obligations were practically nonexistent. Chiune was especially pleased that they no longer had to attend diplomatic functions. He enjoyed spending the long Baltic evenings with his family. About a half year after arriving in Kaunas, their third son was born in April of 1940. Because he was a child of spring they named him Haruki, which means Spring Child as well as bright child. Just as Hiroki affectionately became known as Puppe among family members, Haruki soon became known affectionately as Kuri-chan. Kuri-chan meant Little Chestnut. Everyone in the family agreed that his head looked like a little brown chestnut. By then, Chiaki, their second son was being called Chi-chan. Chi-chan was a diminutive form of his given name, Chiaki.

Chiune had a tendency to develop habits and routines. His day usually began early in the morning. Each morning, he started his day by working in the lower level basement area of the Consulate. That area was set aside as his official office. He spent most of the morning working there and would later join the family for lunch. It was not an especially active consulate. Only a few people a day would

The Consulate building in Kaunas. Within a few months after this picture was taken, hundreds of Jewish refugees would be converging in front of the gates.

visit the Consulate to get information and to apply for visas. The Consulate had a five member staff who worked in various different capacities. They had a housekeeper, a cook, a chauffeur, and two office staff members. One member of the office staff was Borislav and the other member was Gudje. Their roles as office staff members were never clearly defined. Chiune referred to Borislav as the Consulate butler. There were speculations that they were both there for the purpose of helping Chiune with his intelligence work. Borislav was apparently Polish and Gudje, was German. Gudje was sent from Berlin to work with Chiune in Kaunas. The Sugihara children loved Gudje because he played with them and taught them how to speak German. Although an imposing figure, he was kind and gentle to the children. However, suspicions persisted about him being a German agent sent to Kaunas for the purpose of keeping an eye on Chiune's activities.

A very friendly and attractive lady named Miss Uldivyte and her brother lived on the upper floor of the building. At that time, they were both students at a nearby university. The Sugihara family had a friendly relationship with Miss Uldivyte. Hiroki, the eldest son remembers going upstairs to visit her often because he liked to look out of her large front window. That window afforded the best view of people going by and about activities that were going on in the street below. Much later in the 1990s, when tourist came to visit the old Consulate, Miss Uldivyte was still living there. When the visitors inquired about Chiune living there many years ago, she would point to a tree in the yard and say, "Yes, I remember that he was a very kind and handsome man. That tree over there is the one that he himself planted." Miss Uldivyte passed away in the year 2000.

The family remembers that Chiune often took the family for drives and picnics to different places in the countryside. For the children, it was a very special treat. Much later, they realized that those excursions into the country were also opportunities for Chiune to check out different nearby, and often some faraway places. In retrospect, Hiroki and Yukiko remembered that during those trips, Chiune would go off on his own and disappear for hours. At the time, Yukiko was not overly concerned because she had discovered that her husband had inclinations towards eccentric behavior. For example, she remembered the scare he caused in Helsinki. It happened in the middle of the night, when the chauffeur discovered that the Consulate vehicle was missing. Just recently, Chiune had decided to take driving lessons from the chauffeur. After a few lessons, he felt confident that he could drive by himself. However, he never got an opportunity to try because the chauffeur drove them everywhere. One night, he decided to take a test drive while everyone was asleep. When the chauffeur discovered that the car was missing, he immediately went to notify Chiune. Of course, Chiune was not to be found anywhere. Yukiko and the chauffeur became frantic and were looking all over for him when he drove up into the driveway. With a broad smile and a self satisfied expression on his face, he said, "I had a very good drive by myself tonight." Since arriving in Kaunas, Yukiko had also noticed that Chiune would frequently suddenly disappear for a while, and then suddenly return as though nothing had happened. It isn't surprising that Yukiko paid no particular attention to Chiune's activities or regarded anything he did as being unusual.

The fact of the matter is that even during these family trips, Chiune would go off alone in areas where he would take special notes about unusual activities. He would look for signs of sudden changes in the population. For example, if a certain area seemed to have a sudden decrease in the male population, he might take it as an indication that they were being drafted into the army. He looked for unusual tracks in the ground that might indicate that military vehicles passed through. He took into account unusually heavy grooves on the roads that may have been made by trucks carrying heavy loads. He would also report on buildups of new structures and take note of unusual changes in the landscape. He recorded activities on the waterways and noted the kinds of cargo or types of boats that were observed. Chiune understood by now that although his assignment to Kaunas was supposedly to open up a new consulate, he realized the reality was that he was sent for the special mission of making intelligence reports about activities in that region. Lithuania was an ideal location for his intelligence activities because it bordered the Soviet Union, Poland, Latvia, the Baltic Sea and German territories. It was an ideal place to keep an eye on German and Soviet activities. The fact that he had acquired fluency in German, Russian, and English was an additional factor that influenced his superiors to decide that he was the best candidate for this mission.

A photo taken during their outings in Kaunas. Seated with Chiune is Haruki and sitting in front is Hiroki.

Japan believed it was necessary to monitor German movements and to know exactly what they were doing before deciding to sign a pact with Germany. When the Molotov-Ribbentrop Agreement was signed in August of 1939, Japan believed it was a violation of the Anti-Comintern Pact of 1937. There were two factions in the Japanese government; those that were pro-German, and the other was the pro-western faction. As stated earlier, Chiune leaned towards the latter group. The pro-German group was lead by Ambassador Oshima, who was getting closer towards accomplishing his goal, to strengthen ties with Germany. His faction had the majority of the power of the army behind them. However, there were others in the pro-German faction that considered an alliance with Germany as an "uneasy alliance", or it was even described as just a "hollow alliance." They thought that it was most important to check out and confirm information that they were receiving from Germans about their activities in the eastern section of Europe. Despite the fact that the Ribbentrop-Molotov non-aggression pact had been signed quite recently, there were rumors and suspicions that Germany would eventually invade the Soviet Union. Confirmation of that intelligence was very crucial for Japan who had thousands of troops guarding Soviet territory in Manchuria. If Germany were to invade the Soviet Union, the Soviets would find it necessary to deploy their troops from the Manchurian borders to their western fronts in order to defend

Yukiko mentioned a frequent visitor referred to as The Crow. The individual pictured with Chiune is believed to be the frequent visitor who might have been involved with intelligence.

themselves from the Germans. That, in turn would free Japanese troops from guarding the Manchurian borders. The Japanese were anxious to deploy those troops to the Pacific because that was where Japanese military buildup was currently being concentrated.

Chiune's intelligence work was not only confined to making reports about his trips into the countryside of Lithuania. The presence of Borislav and Gudje was also an indication of further intelligence activity in the Kaunas Consulate. Yukiko often referred to a frequent visitor in her memoir. She mentioned that he would often stay for prolonged periods of time. She indicated that he was called The Crow because of his dark, swarthy features. Chiune implied that he was an informant. Yukiko never became well acquainted with The Crow and never found out the reasons for his frequent mysterious visits. She also remembered two other frequent visitors who were later identified as members of the Polish underground.

Japan's cooperation with the Polish underground goes back as far as the 1920s when Poland defeated the Soviet Union in the Polish-Russian War of 1920. It is believed that Japan and Poland jointly deciphered Russian coded messages. The Poles were extremely clever in cracking codes. They were credited with cracking

German codes during WWII. Chiune was known to collaborate with two Polish operatives. They were Lt. Leszek Daszkiewicz and Captain Alfons Jakubianic; Chiune referred to them as Kuba and Daszkiewicz. Another interesting point that should be duly noted was that Sugihara's orders were to report directly to Tokyo rather than to Berlin. Generally, intelligence activities in Europe were under the authority of the Berlin office; which was then, under the direction of Ambassador Oshima. The interesting fact that belies this fact is that it was an unusual change from the prescribed routine to report to Tokyo instead of to Berlin. It also raises the question of how much authority did Ambassador Oshima really have over Chiune Sugihara. Although it is believed that he was indirectly involved in the decision to send Chiune to Kaunas, because of his success in convincing Japan to form an alliance with Germany, questions remain as to why Chiune's orders were to report to Tokyo and not to Berlin. Another interesting fact that may not have any particular relevance to anything, is the fact that both Chiune and Ambassador Oshima came from Gifu Prefecture. This fact is mentioned because in Japanese personal relationships and often in political connections, there are tendencies for those who come from similar locations to form bonds based often on their home background. Records also exist that report about Chiune's visit to Berlin in September of 1939, a month before his move to Lithuania. The report indicated that the purpose for his trip was to purchase a safety deposit box and to receive secret codes at the Japanese Embassy. However, there are no known records of Sugihara meeting with Oshima at that time.

The fact of Chiune's participation and collaboration with the Polish underground also raises some very important questions that bring up some intriguing facts. The person in charge of intelligence in Europe was General Makoto Onodera. He disliked Hitler and was a strong detractor for any ideas about forming an alliance with Germany. He was a proponent for developing better relations with the west or was considered to be pro-western. Chiune was also pro-western and shared similar views with General Onodera. General Onodera had great confidence in information received from the Poles and relied heavily on their intelligence. He had received information from Kuba, Daszkiewicz, and other Polish intelligence operatives that he considered as valuable information. It concerned information about a concentration of the German army in East Germany (Prussia). That information pointed to an important clue. It helped to bolster Japan's suspicion of Germany's intent to invade the Soviet Union. Chiune's orders were to work with the two Poles and to further investigate their findings in order to confirm their authenticity. Chiune's relationship with Polish Intelligence also grew out of the fact that when Germany occupied Poland, the Polish Consulate closed down in protest. They protested the fact that Polish territory in and around Vilnius had been handed over to Lithuania. As a result, the Polish intelligence service became involved in helping displaced Polish refugees. That situation eventually led to the Japanese Consulate getting involved with the Polish intelligence service. These factors help to explain how Chiune began his collaboration with Polish intelligence and with his two Polish intelligence officers.

In light of these facts, it becomes clearer as to why Sugihara became so cooperative with the Poles. It was also well known that General Onodera, who worked from the Swedish Embassy did a lot to help the Jewish refugees. He was later actively involved in helping to bring about a speedier end to Japan's continuation in the war. After the war, Sugihara and Onodera maintained correspondence with each other.

In order to facilitate working with the two Poles, Sugihara found jobs for both Kuba and Daszkiewicz in his Kaunas Consulate. He provided their cover by appointing them to be as Consulate secretaries and couriers. Under the guise of being couriers for the Japanese Foreign Ministry, they were able to travel with relative freedom through Europe on his official car with their Japanese passes. His collaboration with the Polish operatives helped Chiune to obtain vital and important information for Japan. The key information concerned information about when Germany would attack Russia. Chiune also helped with the transfer of a package containing information to Major Michael Rybikowski, another Polish intelligence officer in Stockholm. This package was eventually sent to the Polish government official in exile in London. When Sugihara left Kaunas, his two Polish officers followed him to Berlin.

While all these activities produced an atmosphere of intrigue within the Consulate, great changes in Europe were also taking place that affected thousands of lives. Lithuania had been designated as an independent state and Jews escaping Poland regarded it as a place of refuge. Then suddenly, without any warning, Lithuania became annexed to the Soviet Union. Prior to the annexation, thousands of Polish Jews had recently fled to independent Lithuania, when Germany had first invaded Poland. They believed that it was a place of refuge where they could be protected from being killed or to be protected from being put into concentration camps. With annexation of Lithuania from the Soviets, they now faced the specter of being put away in Siberian slave camps by the Soviets. There were no avenues of escape for the Jews. There were roadblocks and barbed wire fences to prevent escape. Opportunities for escape, whether from air, sea, or land was impossible. Any attempts to escape via the Baltic Sea were also futile because gunboats and submarines blocked the way. All of these circumstances were leading up to an encounter that involved thousands of Jewish refugees and a lone Japanese Vice Consul in Kaunas, Lithuania.

THE REFUGEES

"Even a hunter cannot kill a bird that comes to him for refuge."
Chinese proverb stated by Chiune Sugihara

It was on an early morning, a little past mid July, when the life of the Sugihara Family changed forever. The short summer days were already becoming shorter. It was an indication of an early fall. It was usual for the long and cold winter to come too quickly in those Baltic countries. Being an early riser, Chiune prepared to wake up at his regular morning hour. He woke up at his usual time that day late in July. It was well before the time that the rest of the family got up. However, that morning was different. He became aware of sounds below their bedroom window. It had the distinct sound of a large group of people. He cautiously peeked out of the window and was astounded by the scene that met his eyes. There below him were over a hundred people who were apparently waiting for the Consulate to open. The Consulate usually had two or three visitors a day, so it came as a shock for him to see so many people below. Unsure of the true nature of the situation and the reason why they were there, he quickly woke Yukiko. He instructed her to gather the family together and even suggested hiding in the closet until he found out what was happening. He managed to gather his staff together and gave them instructions to stay inside. Over the growing roar of the crowd, he was able to discern that the people below were speaking Polish and Yiddish. He sent Borislav, his Polish staff member, to find out why they were there.

Borislav returned and explained that they were mostly Jews. Some of them had walked nearly 80 miles from the nearby city of Vilnius (Wilno) to Kaunas. He explained that when the Poles had made their initial escape from Poland following Germany's occupation, many of them had fled to Vilnius. Vilnius was a city with a very large Jewish population of approximately 20,000 Polish refugees. The complete Jewish population in Vilnius numbered nearly 100,000. Vilnius had been inhabited by Jews since the 16th Century and eventually became a center of Jewish culture. Most of the Jews had fled from Poland when Germans had occupied their land. Upon hearing what Borislav reported, it quickly became very clear to Chiune the reason why those people had suddenly come in such great numbers to his Consulate. He himself had just been recently made aware of the fact that the Soviets had taken over Lithuania and he had also been given orders to vacate the Consulate and to leave as soon as possible. His order was to take a train to Berlin to receive his next assignment. Since the family had grown from four, to six people, packing was difficult and it took more time. Most of the other Consuls in Kaunas had vacated their Consulates as soon as they were asked to leave by the Russians. Had these people standing at Chiune's Consulate gate come any later, the Sugiharas would have been packed and well on their way to Berlin. So the miracle was that because the Sugihara family's packing was delayed, they were still there when the refugees arrived. It was truly a stroke of luck for them that the Japanese Consulate was in fact, still open. He also remembered that it had just been over a half year ago, when the family had attended a Hannukah party. A young boy named Solly Ganor and Chiune had met in Solly's aunt's gourmet shop. Chiune had offered to give Solly some Hannukah gelt money so that he could see the latest Laurel and Hardy film. In return, Solly had invited the Vice Consul to the family's Hannukah dinner. To the great surprise and pleasure of the family, Sugihara actually arrived with his whole family. It was a memorable experience. Chiune thought about what he had heard from relatives and friends who had just recently arrived from Poland. He recalled how they had tearfully described the ordeals and hardships that they endured in Poland and about the difficulties that they encountered during their escape from Poland. Chiune understood that all of these people were now actually refugees and that they were trapped like mice with virtually no avenue of escape. He realized that to those refugees at the gate, he was essentially their last hope for any chance of escape because his Consulate still happened to be open. Vilnius or any other location in Soviet occupied Lithuania was not a safe place for them since that area of Lithuania had just been taken over by the Russians. He understood that since routes to the west were all closed, the only possible route for escape would be across Russia and then through Japan. He was also aware that because Japan was presently involved in negotiations concerning the formation of a pact with Germany, they would never agree to do anything that would jeopardize finalizing that pact. Despite the fact that he clearly understood the situation and realized that there was little he could do to help them, Chiune Sugihara agreed to listen to five chosen representatives and invited them to tell him of their desperate situation.

Most of the people waiting at the gate were Polish Jews. But who led them there? What were all the circumstances that led to their being at Vice Consul Sugihara's doorstep? Was it a matter of luck or some other acts of fate? Was it their individual resolve to not accept defeat and to utilize everything within their grasp to insure their survival? What were the factors that determined that over 6000 individuals escaped with their lives and evaded capture or unspeakable horrors? Each one's story is different, but they are all significant. Despite the fact that 65 years have passed since then, the stories and accounts from survivors remind us that we should never forget what happened and to try to learn a lesson from what they share. Testimonies from the actual survivors or stories handed down by the survivor's to their descendants provide us with their incredible sagas of survival. It is incredible that it is still possible today, to hear first hand, accounts of what the factors were that made each survival possible. The remembrances of these survivors also enable historians and those curious about this terrible time in our history, to get a more complete perspective of what happened during those dark days called the Holocaust.

Through these individual accounts, we can peer into the past and recapture the drama and pathos of what actually took place. We can try to put ourselves into the situation that Consul Sugihara was confronted with when he agreed to meet the refugees. We can judge for ourselves, how we may have reacted if we were under the pressures that Chiune found himself. Perhaps we may be able to better understand the courage it took for Chiune to say, "I had no choice but to do something, because it was just the right thing to do." Although some memories have faded, an astounding number of survivors vividly remember it clearly. It is fortunate that we can try to piece together some of the stories so that we can get a clearer picture of what happened during those difficult times. We can try to relive the drama of that time and to also try to imagine the emotions that must have prevailed. To insure that future generations remember these stories, they must try to become involved both mentally and emotionally as they read or listen to the testimonies of these survivors. The remembering and retelling of these stories provides a lesson about the meanings of words like tenacity, determination, perseverance, intuitiveness, and all the other words that describe the traits that it took to survive in the face of overwhelming odds.

GEORGE LIEBERT (LIEBERFREUND)

George Liebert's story is our first testimony. George is known as, "the man in the crowd," because his picture is most prominent in the famous Sugihara photo of the crowd at the Consulate gate. But George is more than the man pictured in the crowd, he is a living symbol of why Sugihara's gift was so precious. The fact that George Liebert is alive and well today, is just another wondrous story and can qualify as a miracle. In fact, George himself is a living miracle. George is currently 93 years of age and lives in the middle of the affluent part of Manhattan in New York City. He speaks and behaves like a very genteel and worldly gentleman who was brought up with the awareness of good manners and has the air of a man of the world. He knows how to read and speak at least five languages. Those who know George well will give fair warning to anyone meeting George for the first time. They will say, "Don't expect to meet someone that you imagine to be a 93 years old man, expect to meet someone who is more like 70 years old."

George Liebert, standing in the middle of the crowd on July 27, 1940. George was 30 years old when he received his Sugihara visa.

It was Aunt Setsuko, Yukiko's sister, who took that famous photo that helped to verify what the Sugihara family remembered about the crowd coming at their gate on that July morning in 1940. The fact that George Liebert is still alive and can attest to the facts remembered by the Sugiharas, adds more credence to their story and provides concrete evidence about its validity. The first miracle that is connected with the photo is that it really does exist today when the fact is that all of the Sugihara's photos were originally confiscated from them. When the Russians captured them as prisoners of war, they confiscated everything owned by the family. However, Yukiko was able to talk one of the soldiers into returning precious family photos. Miraculously, among those photos were two pictures about the crowd at their gate. That is the only reason why the pictures still remain today. In that one and only clear photo was George Liebert, standing prominently in the middle of the crowd, wearing a light colored trench coat. The second miracle connected with the picture is that George Liebert was located. And the third wonderful part is that George Liebert remembers many things about that time and shares his vivid memories.

It is most likely that the picture of the crowd was taken on July 27, 1940, because George's visa was stamped on that date. That photo also verifies that the crowd had already formed at the gate by that date. We can also verify the fact that George Liebert (Lieberfreund), was one of the early recipients of the Sugihara visa because he received Visa number 30. The reason why George Liebert happened to be at the Japanese Consul's gate so early is another amazing story.

By age 30, the age that George appeared at the gate, he had already completed his education at the University of Bordeau, in France. He graduated from the university with a degree in chemical engineering. His first language was Polish, but he had also spoken French and German because those languages were also prevalent in Poland since Poland had been ruled by kings of those nations or had been part of other nations during their past history. He returned to his native Poland after completing his education in order to help his father run his lucrative glass factory. The factory was located in Krakow, a beautiful southern city of Poland that bordered Germany. In Krakow, his family manufactured beautiful crystal beveled glass. They lived in an opulent residence where the walls were covered with priceless paintings and the home furnished with fine furniture and carpets. However, all this changed in September of 1939, when Germany attacked Poland. Overnight, the Liebert family was reduced to being homeless where just a day before, they had been living in luxury. George was able to get a small car and loaded his mother, father, brother and himself and headed for some destination that afforded them with more safety than that of remaining in Poland could have provided. Their journey of escape included being stopped and questioned for being spies, mixing alcohol with gas to augment their fuel supply, to running for their lives into a forest when airplanes sighted their car and began machine gunning it. They finally arrived in Lwow, where it was considered to be relatively safe. However, his family encouraged George to leave as soon as possible and to seek a way to escape Europe and to contact them if he somehow found a way out. George left his family somewhere near Lwow and headed towards the Baltic Sea area.

George's first focus was to somehow get to Sweden because it was still a neutral state. However, he met with his brother in law who already had a visa to go to the United States. His brother in law told him of a rumor that he had heard about the possibility that one might be able to get a visa from the Dutch Consulate in Kaunas to some remote islands near the United States. At this point, the chance to get any kind of visa was paramount because it provided the best possibility for escape. That rumor is what led George Liebert to the Dutch Consulate and to his meeting with Jan Zwartendijk. Jan Zwartendijk happened to notice George standing near his Consulate because he was one of the first ones there. By chance he asked him if he could read and write French. It was a lucky day for the both of them because for George, French was just like his first language. To this day, George remembers every word that Zwartendijk dictated to him to write in French for his Dutch visa. Copies of what George wrote were made and he was paid five dollars for his work along with receiving a Dutch Curacao-Surinam visa. The Honorary Dutch Consul, Zwartendijk, had just received permission to issue Curacao visas from the Dutch ambassador in Riga, Latvia. His instructions were that it must be written in French. In the following pages, more will be forthcoming about the Dutch-Japanese connection. It was again one of those small miracles that George was there at the Dutch Consulate on that particular day, and was given the unique task of writing in French what the Dutch Consul dictated.

George was also able to clarify a misconception about how the visas were issued. According to him, he was in line waiting to get his visa because someone was probably instructed by Sugihara to collect documents such as identification papers from individuals standing in line outside of the gate area. The person who collected the information then brought a packet of the gathered information into the Consulate. They were all returned to them after Vice Consul Sugihara placed his official seal and signature on them. George estimates that he waited about an hour to get his Sugihara visa and the rest of his identification papers returned to him. It is presumed that, that was the procedure that was chosen by the Vice Consul so that the process of handling and issuing the visas would be as efficient as possible.

Another very interesting fact that was provided by George Liebert is that he was standing at the gate because it was as close to the Consulate as he could get, for an important reason. The reason for why he was facing away from the crowd and looking towards the Consulate when the picture was taken is because he did not want to be recognized or identified by the Russian secret service agents. They were out there threatening to incarcerate them if caught in suspicious activities. According to George, they were attempting to take photos of the people out there for identification purposes. George did not want his picture taken should he ever be turned into the authorities and be identified as someone at the Japanese Consulate. Being one of the oldest survivors who remembers these small, but important details about that time from the past, George is truly a living miracle and a unique individual.

Again through a series of right moves and maneuvers, George survived getting through Siberia, landing safely into Japan. He spent about one year in Japan and finally went to Shanghai. While in Shanghai, the French Consulate recognized that he met the qualifications that enabled him to be like a naturalized French citizen, so he was able to live out side of the Hongkew area of Shanghai where all of the refugees were confined under Japanese authority. Because of his credentials as a chemist, he was able to get employment from a French company that produced a milk-like product that used soy as a base, and worked as a chemist for them. Due to all of those circumstances, George was able to get an apartment in a fairly nice neighborhood and earn a modest living as a chemist in Shanghai. George Liebert remained in Shanghai for over six years and was released after the end of WWII. He was released from Shanghai in 1948, and arrived in the United States in 1949. He was a penniless survivor who again had to find a way to survive in this new land.

The fate of his parents and brother who had escaped out of Krakow was a different story. They were eventually captured by the Russians and sent to Siberia in the far backwoods of that land and placed in what can be described as a Siberian slave labor camp. His brother was considered an enemy of Russia and sentenced to a 25 years and was released after serving 20 years. His parents were released six years later and they returned to Poland. During one of the anti-Semitic pogroms organized by Polish people, 40 Jews were murdered; one of the victims was George's father. George was able to get his mother to the United States in 1960. He cared for her for several decades until she passed away. Today, George will tell anyone who will listen, "For me, everyday is Thanksgiving. Israel may be the country of my heart, but the United States is the Promised Land."

RABBI SAMUEL ISIDORE (ISAAC) GRAUDENZ

Rabbi Graudenz is 88 years old and he presently lives in San Francisco in an assisted living home. Despite the fact that his sight is somewhat impaired because of complications connected with macular degeneration, he is still a very vigorous individual and has all the earmarks of a survivor. Some of his memories of the past have faded, however, his daughter, Debby Graudenz, provides details that he no longer remembers well. His colleagues and those who know him well affectionately call him Isi. One of the unique facts about Rabbi Graudenz was that he was among the group that arrived in Kaunas from Vilnius with Dr. Zorach Warhaftig and was among the five representatives that were invited by Consul Sugihara to explain about their desperate plight. Rabbi Graudenz' relationship with Dr. Warhaftig goes back to the time when as a brilliant teen aged rabbinical student, he met Dr. Warhaftig. They were paired off as study partners at the renowned center of Jewish learning, the Mir Yeshiva, in Mir, Poland. Dr. Warhaftig, 10 years his senior, was actually Rabbi Graudenz' teacher. He had long been an ardent proponent of the Zionist cause and became an active member of the Zionist movement in Vilnius. When they met again in Vilnius, Rabbi Graudenz was invited by Dr. Warhaftig to serve as the group's interpreter because besides speaking several languages, he also spoke English.

Dr. Warhaftig can be considered as one of the most influential and charismatic leaders in the Zionist movement. Under his zeal and leadership, he is given credit for leading the majority of the survivors to Sugihara's doorstep. He later became one of the signatories of Israel's Scroll of Independence and a leading member of the Knesset until 1981. From 1962 to 1974, he served as Minister of Religious Affairs and was regarded as one of the highest authorities of Hebrew Law. Dr. Warhaftig passed away in the year of 2003. The goal of the religious or orthodox Zionist movement was to ultimately reach their haven, to Eretz Yisrael, to make Aliyah.

Rabbi Graudenz received Visa number 330, issued on July 30, 1940. His life story is an incredible one where his first significant memories began at an orphanage in Dinslaken, Germany. As a youngster of only five and a half years of age, his parents made the decision to send him to the orphanage. They realized that they had an especially gifted son. Appreciating the fact that their young offspring had great potential as a scholar, they made the decision that he had a better chance to develop his potential in an orphanage. Realizing that a much better educational environment existed in the orphanage, they gave him up after they were given a recommendation by a Jewish social service network to have Samuel put under the care of an orphanage. Since Samuel's parents had left Poland for Germany, they had found that it was extremely difficult to make ends meet and to adequately provide for a growing family. Some of his other siblings were also given up to other orphanages. With the exception of a son named Max, who died during childhood, all the other six children miraculously escaped the Nazis. However, it was only Samuel who entered the kindersheim (children's home) in Dinslaken. The Jewish social service recommendation proved to be accurate because he thrived very well there and excelled academically. He was a brilliant student at the renowned rabbinical school, Hildesheimer Seminary, in Berlin. He accomplished an incredible feat by completing his training there at the remarkably young age of 21. Samuel never received German citizenship because his parents were Polish citizens. In 1938, when Germany evicted all Polish subjects from Germany, he was sent back to Poland. When Germany occupied Poland in 1939, Rabbi Graudenz, along with hundreds of others, fled to Vilnius where he was reunited with Dr. Warhaftig, a leader of the religious Zionist movement. Dr. Warhaftig clearly understood how urgent it was for Jews to get out of Europe. He was investigating all possibilities and explored any options that may have existed to find ways to get out of Europe.

He was relentless in seeking a way out and left no stone unturned in his pursuit. When he heard about the Japanese Consul in Kaunas, he went to investigate. He noted all the information that he could obtain and came up with the conclusion that there might exist a small window of opportunity for a plan of escape from Kaunas. Dr. Warhaftig, Rabbi Graudenz, and other leaders of the Zionist movement followed Dr. Warhaftig to Kaunas, Lithuania. This was the scenario that precipitated the exodus of thousands from Vilnius to Kaunas.

Rabbi Graudenz was one of those thousands and was at the gate of the Japanese Vice Consul on that early morning in July. Rabbi Graudenz' account of their encounter with Chiune Sugihara reveals a heartwarming scenario. He recollected that the Consulate was also the Sugihara family home and remembers the gracious hospitality of Chiune Sugihara. Rabbi Graudenz' important role during these discussions was that he translated into Polish, the English that Chiune chose to speak during the meeting. In one instance, he recalls even playing with the Chiune's children on the floor of their living quarters. After the representatives finished telling Vice Consul Sugihara about their desperate situation, he remembered that Sugihara was deeply moved. Chiune responded by saying, "I will try to help as many of you as I can." He remembered that because the Vice Consul's concern was so sincere, they left that first meeting with a sense of renewed hope.

A very interesting statement that Rabbi Graudenz made during one of his interviews concerns the question of who came up with the idea of using a Curacao stamp in order to fulfill the requirement needed for Sugihara to issue his transit visas. Rabbi Graudenz stated that the idea came from Chiune Sugihara. If the Rabbi's recollection is accurate, it also helps to bolster the evidence that two Polish officers who worked for him had reported that fact also. The original idea could have been devised between Chiune, and his two Polish intelligence officers, Kuba and Daszkiewicz during the course of one of their discussion. It is plausible that after the first meeting with the five representatives, Sugihara met with the Poles and described to them, in great detail, about the plight of the refugees. The fact that prior to the refugee's arrival, Vice Consul Sugihara had already issued over 60 visas in the early part of July is important because he must have come across a Dutch visa prior to his decision to issue thousands more. It is certain that when he signed the visa # 30, for George Liebert, he must have noticed the inclusion of the Curacao-Surinam visa then. The idea for using Curacao stamps could have come to his mind when he remembered seeing a Curacao stamp on one of those previous visas and remembered the words stating that Visas were not required for entry to Curacao-Surinam Islands. It is also very likely, that it was in fact, an idea that came up during the course of his discussion with the Poles.

Apparently, after the initial meeting, several other discussions were held at the Consulate. Yukiko recalls that the Dutch interim Consul, Jan Zwartendijk visited the Consulate and attended one of the later meetings. Although there are conflicting accounts about whose idea it was to use Curacao as an end destination, the important point is that such an idea was devised. It would be a moot point to try to determine whose idea it was. The important facts are that the Dutch vice consul kindly agreed to cooperate and that Chiune Sugihara made the decision to courageously go against his government's orders in order to issue life saving visas. The creative resourcefulness, foresight and perseverance of Dr. Warhaftig, Rabbi Graudenz, and others of like mind were the catalysts needed to encourage others to persist. Ultimately, their determination and tenacity enabled over 6000 individuals to receive their life saving visas.

After Rabbi Graudenz received his precious Sugihara visa, he had other obstacles to overcome. He had his Curacao destination visa, his Sugihara transit visa and a violin. That violin was what provided him with the third thing he needed to escape to Japan, thereby, enabling him to save his life. That third thing was a ticket to get on the Trans-Siberian Railroad train to go across Siberia to Vladivostok and finally to Japan. He did not have the money to buy that ticket, but he did have his precious violin that he had received from the orphanage. He had become quite an accomplished violinist and loved to play it often. It was difficult for him to decide to part with his violin, but Rabbi Graudenz realized that it was the only thing of value that he owned. He decided that he must use his violin in exchange for a train ticket. A passing Russian soldier noticed his violin and promised that he would return the next day with a ticket. Having no other choice but to take a chance with this soldier, he agreed to the barter. On the following day when the soldier miraculously appeared with his ticket, he made the vow to give up what he loved best to do; that was, that he would never play the violin again. Many years later in 1997, when speaking about Sugihara, Rabbi Graudenz said, " He was a messenger sent from God. Had it not been for Sugihara, I would not be here today."

THE ISAAC MELAMED (MELAMDOVICH) FAMILY

Isaac Melamdovich brought his family to the gates of the Consulate in early August. He had brought along his wife Faygl, and eight years old son, Leo (Leibl). They came from the town of Bialystok, a small city in northeast Poland and midway between Warsaw and Vilnius. Their son, Leo, an intelligent and very impressionable young man was born in Bialystok in 1932. Isaac was a teacher at Grosser Shul. It was an elementary school whose entire curriculum was conducted in Yiddish. Isaac was a mathematics teacher who had written the mathematics textbooks that was adopted by all the Yiddish schools. As a descendant of the family of Melamed (Melamdovich), which means family of teachers, it was appropriate that he chose to be a teacher. He was an intellectual with progressive ideas. In fact, one could describe him as a visionary. Like many intellectuals like him, he had a vision for Poland where her inhabitants would someday enjoy equal economic, educational, religious, political, social, and civil rights. He believed that for the Jews in Poland to be recognized as part of the official citizenry of Poland, Jewish culture had to establish their cultural autonomy. He believed that in order to establish that autonomy, secular, rather than religious teachings had to be firmly established. Many intellectuals like Isaac, believed that Jews must be freed from religious dogmas that had been handed down for generations. They felt that by denouncing the old religious tenets and customs, it would help forge the realization of Jewish emancipation. Because Isaac believed that religious dogma discouraged intellectual development and higher levels of understanding, he chose to be an agnostic. It was considered a very radical idea for those times. Isaac believed that the acceptance of Yiddish as an official or national language of the people would be the most important goal to be accomplished towards realizing Jewish cultural autonomy. The reason for his belief was the fact that he believed that it was language that tied people together. It was the glue that defined their ethnicity, history, arts, and culture. If the goal of attaining Jewish autonomy became a reality, many members of the intelligentsia envisioned that it would be followed by great improvements in all aspects of life for the working class. The people who advocated for these progressive reforms were called the Bund or the Bundist Movement. It was essentially a party for the working class or the socialist party. Isaac Melamdovich was an important leader of this group in his town of Bialystok. There were groups throughout Europe that advocated for better conditions for the working class and were referred to as the Bundist movement. While the Zionist's goal was a return to Eretz Yisrael, the Bundists believed in making a stand within their adopted countries and to fight for their civil rights as rightful Polish citizens.

His wife Faygl was a teacher who also taught at Grosser Shul, at the elementary level. She was also ahead of her times and considered as an emancipated woman. Being a woman of the intelligentsia, she was out-spoken and zealously supported and joined with her husband in spreading the ideals about revolutionizing the thinking of the citizenry. She was a highly regarded teacher and was at ease and confident, as she joined in the many intellectual discussions that Isaac Melamdovich often held at his home. Faygl was an attractive woman, all the more so, because she exuded a positive presence. Despite her career-oriented focus, she was a very nurturing person and a loving mother. She and Leo, her only child experienced many adventures together. They bonded together in a special way as children with "good" mothers often do. She was an accomplished teacher and one of those kinds of teachers that children tend to remember because she touched her students in special ways. During their perilous escape out of Europe, her presence was a definite advantage to Isaac because she had spunk and adapted well to the unpredictable situations that they faced during those arduous and challenging times. Leo, their only child of eight years, also was a unique individual. He was blessed with two wonderful parents. Isaac, the father, always the teacher, never missed a chance to enlighten Leo. Whether it was about math, science, or geography; it all depended on whatever environment they found themselves in; Isaac managed to take advantage of the situation. He always capitalized upon a situation and found a way to use the moment as a teaching tool. For example, if they were in ice cold, 40 degrees below zero temperature in Siberia, he would teach Leo how to convert fahrenheit to centigrade. On the other hand, Faygl, his mother was more practical and as mentioned before, very nurturing. While Isaac was uncomfortable about expressing affection, Faygl, more than made up for Isaac's lack. Leo, or Leibl, as he was called then, felt more comfortable in the company of adults rather than with other children. Being an only child, he was usually in the company of adults. To this day, Leo has fond memories of living with his grandmother (Babba) and his beautiful Aunt Bobble; both were killed at Groyse Shul, a synagogue in Bialystok. The synagogue was admired as one of the beautiful examples of old-world architecture that combined Prussian and Russian influences. Tragically, on July 27, 1941, the Germans rounded up the Jewish citizenry of Bialystok into Groyse Shul, covered the architecturally magnificent edifice with gasoline, ignited it, and killed all the occupants within. The synagogue and everyone in it perished. The family of Isaac Melamdovich, were the only survivors of their family in Bialystok.

Later in his memoir titled, "Escape to the Futures," Leo describes a scene that took place in 1940. While traveling on the Trans Siberian train, during the arduous and treacherous trip across the frigid, vast Siberian tundra, the game of chess was being played before his eyes. Never mind that at any moment, the train could stop and his father could be identified as a fugitive and taken away to a Siberian slave camp. The only thing that mattered then was that game of chess. The drama that was going on between his father and his opponent, an old brooding, long-bearded man, taught Leo a lesson about life. As an eight years old child, he was very impressionable. As he observed his father playing chess, he learned something about playing the game of life. He realized that playing the game of chess is much like living life. He observed that first you need a plan, a strategy. Next, you need to be focused, patient, and have good timing. But included in this mix was that one special ingredient, intuition. One needed to trust one's intuition and to know when to use it. It is unlikely that Leo understood all of this instantly, but over time, he never forgot that scene. Observing his father make his calculated moves, strongly impressed him and left a definite imprint on his life. Watching his father engaged in the game also gave him a clue as to why they had managed to escape so far.

Isaac Melamdovich received Visa number 1768. Faygl Melamdovich, with her son Leibl, received Visa number 1758. They both received it on August 14, 1940. Although there were only two visas issued, it covered three individuals. To clarify how it worked would be that for example, if a mother had three children, she would only get one visa with her children's names listed on it, and therefore, one visa would save four individuals. These examples illustrate why it is not possible to find out the exact number of lives that were saved by Chiune Sugihara.

Leo recalls certain impressions and scenes at the Consulate as his family anxiously waited for their turn to enter the premises of the Consulate. He especially remembers the emotions of impatience, anxiety and fear that permeated the atmosphere of the Consulate. Leo's most vivid recollection is the great excitement that his parents expressed when they finally received their visas. The excitement of receiving their visas was however clouded by the realization that they had other obstacles to be met before they were out of harm's way. As city councilman at Bialystok, Isaac had been on the wanted list by the German authorities because he was considered to be a leader of the community. Isaac realized early that when the Germans occupied their town, the town leaders would be imprisoned and held hostage. As a result, he and other Jewish leaders of the community went into hiding. Very shortly, the Russians took over the regions of Bialystok from the Germans. This was a result of a prior agreement between Russia and Germany that they would divide Poland between them. When the leaders heard that the Germans had left, they decided that it would be safe to return. Isaac stubbornly refused to go along with them stating that he could no more trust the Bolsheviks than he could the Nazis. He held strong to his opinion and he became the lone fugitive. The rest of the leaders returned to Bialystok. In a matter of less than a week, those who returned to Bialystok were rounded up and sent to Siberia. They were never heard from again. Being an active member of the Bund , as well as being a leader of the community, he was on the wanted list of groups such as the GPU, the precursor of the KGB, and later by the NKBD. As one of the city councilman of Bialystok, the Gestapo wanted him and all the leaders of the town to be imprisoned as their hostages. If the local citizens violated any of their rules, the hostages would be punished. In other words, the Nazis used them as their pawns. The NKBD had their eyes on him because they regarded him as a leader and spokesperson for the Bund Movement; therefore, he posed a threat to them also. Being wanted from all directions was very risky business, but Isaac proved to be a formidable player and opponent. As the situation in Bialystok became even more intolerable and the realization that he could never return there, set in, Isaac decided that it was time to get his family out of there. The situation became even more urgent when he received information that all the borders between Poland and Lithuania would be closed, and that access by train would no longer be possible. He immediately sent word secretly to Faygl giving her instructions to get both Liebl and her on the last possible train to Vilnius. With their quick coordination and precision in their planning, they safely escaped from Bialystok. They safely reached Vilnius where Isaac awaited them. From that point on, Isaac managed to be at all the right places to hear about the schemes that were going around about how to get out of Europe. When Isaac heard about the Japanese and the Dutch visa scheme, he probably recognized that plan to be a feasible one and immediately led his family to Kaunas. Thus, the Melamdovich family again took another step towards getting closer to escaping Europe with their lives.

After receiving their Sugihara visa, Isaac kept a very low profile and exhibited great discipline in maintaining patience. He was careful to remain close to his family and communicated to them by using secret signals devised by him and Faygl. As a result, he eluded detection. While Isaac hid in different locations, Faygl and Leo waited in Vilnius for their papers to come. Their patience was finally rewarded when the papers came permitting them to go through Russia. During the trip across Siberia, they kept a very low profile by being very discrete, and managed not to attract attention. Isaac Melamdovich again managed to evade capture by consistently staying one step ahead, or anticipating the next move, just as he did while engaged in the game of chess. By utilizing his wile, powers of observation, timing and trusting his intuition, he successfully brought his family out of Europe and reached Japan safely. Incredibly, the State Department of the United States, became aware of the precarious situation of the Melandovich family by the American Federation of Labor. As a result, influence was put upon the Japanese Foreign Ministry to give the family priority to receive visas for entry to the United States. Young Leibl, learned much during his incredible journey to safety. It later became apparent that he had acquired the same kind of tenacity and determination that his father had by successfully meeting the new challenges of living in the United States.

SALOMON BROTHERS

Two brothers, Bernard (Boruch Szmul) and Abram Salomon were also at the Japanese Consulate gate. The younger of the two brothers, Abram had recently graduated from the University of Warsaw and was embarking upon a new career as an attorney when rumors and indications that Poland was no longer safe became more obvious each day. Being within the cosmopolitan atmosphere of the university, he had access to varied opinions and rumors about how best to avoid being caught in the Nazi web. Abram, somehow made a decision to go along with individuals who believed that to head to Vilnius, Lithuania, still an independent state, might be the most viable course of action to take. He made up his mind to go along with that group whose decision was to flee to Vilnius. Abram arrived there on November of 1939. His older brother, Bernard, remained in Warsaw and continued working as an accountant in a bank. Being the oldest son, Bernard felt the responsibility to look over the welfare of his family. When conditions worsened, he returned to Mlava where his family operated a soap factory.

In the meantime, Abram, along with relatives and friends from Warsaw, arrived in Vilnius. There, they came in contact with the religious Zionist groups and others who believed that getting out of Europe should be the priority for anyone who valued their life. Abram began to realize more clearly the precariousness of his safety and became convinced of the reality of the impending dangers that lay in store for Jews. He sensed that serious danger was imminent. With growing alarm, he felt the necessity to do something as soon as possible in order to get out of Europe safely. When he had no doubt about the accuracy of his instinct to flee, he must have immediately contacted his brother, Bernard. Bernard probably trusted and agreed with his brother's concerns.

It is likely that he had a discussion with his parents in Mlava about both their concerns. Bernard apparently decided that he should join his brother in a bid to flee the dangers that continued to increase daily. It is probable that he tried to also convince his parents to leave with him. Whatever their reasons might have been, his parents unfortunately decided to stay in Mlava. Perhaps they believed that things would get better or they could have had apprehensions about whether they were physically capable of meeting the challenges of escaping under the conditions that then prevailed. Bernard, nevertheless, had made his decision to leave Mlava, and to join his brother in Vilnius. Being a young man, he probably thought that taking a chance to escape would be the better option for him. Like his brother Abram, he must have sensed that the situation was getting worse daily and unless he made a move to get out, he would eventually be trapped in Poland with no chance to escape. It is believed that he reluctantly left his home and family because he probably realized that the possibility existed that he would never see his parents again. While there still remained a modicum of time to leave in relative safety, Bernard left hurriedly to join his brother and cousins who were already in Vilnius.

By the time he decided to leave Mlava, it was too late because all the borders between Poland and Lithuania were closed or was in the process of being closed by keeping them under tight control. Although Bernard was correct about his sense of urgency to leave as soon as possible, he was too late. Because the border guards were now keeping tight control over all of the possible escape routes, Bernard was seized and sent to a detention camp where he discerned that his most probable destination and fate would be that he would be sent to a concentration or slave labor camp. His instinct for survival clicked in and enabled him to somehow escape from the detention camp. It is most likely that he stayed hidden until night and under the cover of darkness managed to cut through treacherous barbed wire fences. It is presumed that prior plans had been made as to where he was to meet his brother and cousins. Bernard succeeded in finally reaching a location where brother Abram waited for him with his cousins and a friend. Although all the exact details are not clear, it is probable that his brother, Abram, and his companions were able to successfully coax a border guard to let Bernard through to the other side. The family believes that a bribe was involved in convincing the border guard to agree to cooperate. What was important is that Bernard successfully got through and was able to join his brother, cousins and friend. Joe Salomon, the son of Abram, remarked that knowing his father's ability to convince others to his way of thinking, could have been an important factor in their success towards convincing the guard that night. None of this could have occurred, if the brothers and their cohorts did not possess the qualities that makes every survivor unique. They all seemed to share together the capacity to forge ahead into actions that required courage and daring. They were all willing to take the necessary chances to help each other and themselves. On December of 1939, Bernard successfully crossed the border to unite with his brother.

Thus, the two brothers, Bernard and Abram, eventually became two more people who found themselves at the gate of the Japanese Consulate in Kaunas. Bernard was issued Visa number 299, while Abram was issued Visa number 27. The interesting fact is that Abram received his visa on July 26, 1940, four days before Bernard was issued his visa. The implication here is that right after Abram received his visa, he probably immediately somehow got word to Bernard and the rest of their group about the Sugihara visas because the records show that Bernard, the cousins and the friend received their visas days later. It is presumed that after Bernard's narrow escape to get past the border guards, they spent the next six or seven months living in Vilnius devising plans for further escape through Russia, and then to Japan. Whatever the true circumstances were, the records show that Bernard received his visa four days after Abram received his. Another interesting fact about Abram's visa is that his was # 27. That number indicates that he was one of the first individuals to get his visa. It has never been certain about the individual who was the fifth representative that was invited into the Japanese Consulate. Rumors have persisted that Abram Salomon was one of the leaders of that time. The fact that Abram received Visa # 27, indicates that he was one of the first people to get a visa before Chiune decided to issue visas to the rest of the crowd. These facts add credence to the possibility that Abram was among the leaders of the group. Also, the fact that he was able to get the Curacao-Surinam stamp so quickly, indicates that he could have been privy to first hand information about what was discussed in the Consulate. Abram could also have been the person who passed on the information about the possible usage of the Dutch visa as one that would provide for an end destination. One would almost have to have been at the office to get or give the information concerning the Curacao-Surinam document as quickly as Abram did. Whatever might have been the true situation, there is no doubt that Abram had access to early information and undoubtedly was one of the individuals that went to Kaunas very early in the game. A second interesting point is that before Bernard got his Sugihara visa, he received his stamped Curacao visa on July 27. In other words, he first went to the Dutch Consulate to get his Curacao visa and three days later got his Sugihara visa.

Other important facts substantiated by the Salomon family connection is that Chiune met his goal to issue between 200 to 300 visas a day. The fact that he tried to keep to his promise about issuing visas to as many people as he possibly could, can be verified by checking out the numbers of the visas and the dates when Abram, his brother, Bernard, and cousins of the Salomon family received their visas. For example, Abram received visa # 27, on July 26, and Bernard received his on July 30. It is believed that Sugihara publicly announced that he would issue visas on July 27. People probably came in droves after his announcement. Since Bernard received his visa on July 30, calculating the dates from the time that Abram received his visa and Bernard had received his, Sugihara had issued 272 visas. However, it was after his announcement that he made his vow that word got around that Sugihara decided to issue visas. Then the crowds became larger and Chiune began churning more visas each day. Accompanying the two Salomon brothers throughout most of their journey were cousins named Henry Taca and Bolek Rembaum, and a close friend, Martin Kirshenbaum. There is no doubt that they were all somehow involved in the plan to get Bernard across the border. Their records show that each of them received their visas after Bernard. The cousins Taca and Rembaum received their visas on July 31. Taca received visa # 599, and Rembaum received visa # 576. The records show that between the time that Bernard received his visa #299 and when Taca had received his visa #599, Sugihara had issued 300 visas. Since there is no indication of what time the visas were issued, it is possible that he issued more on that day. Their friend Kirshenbaum received visa #739 on August 1, the following day. The records show that by the time that Kirshenbaum received his visa, Sugihara had already issued 140 visas by the next day. Whether he did it early in the day or later would determine how many more visas he could have actually issued on August 1. The sequencing of the dates that all the cousins and friend received their visas, point out that it is most probable that they got word out to each other about the visas that were being issued by Sugihara. As word got out to them, they apparently individually went to get their visas. All of the individuals involved in the Salomon brothers story proved to be bright, resourceful and resilient young men who demonstrated that a combination of good sense, daring and intelligence were traits needed to survive during those grim times. These young men did escape with their lives, but many of them could not shed the burden and a sense of guilt they carried within because they were forced to leave behind so many family members and friends in Poland. The majority of those who remained in Poland was eventually sent to the Warsaw Ghetto and became victims of Nazi gas chambers. The men who survived are just a sample of the kinds of people who escaped out of Europe. Those characteristics that they exhibited during their daring escapes would later prove to be useful as they met the new challenges that came along in their story of survival.

After finally getting out of Russia via Siberia and crossing the Japan Sea, the Salomon brothers landed safely at Tsuruga Port in Japan. From Japan, their continuing journey was a circuitous odyssey of living and working in various exotic places such as Calcutta, India, Japan, and Australia. Their tenacity and industriousness is evidenced by the fact that they were able to apply and receive visas from Consulates in Argentina, Dominican Republic, Great Britain, India and Egypt. The brothers fully learned their lesson from their experience in Kaunas and appreciated the value of ownership of visas and apparently did not lose any opportunity to acquire a visa whenever it was possible. As part of the Zionist movement, their goal was to eventually reach Palestine. However, because of the closure of the Suez Canal, it was no longer an option. As a result, Bernard lived in Calcutta, India for six years. He worked as an accountant for a tanning factory in Calcutta. During his stay in India, he also became a reporter and wrote articles for a Jewish periodical. His brother went on to Australia where Joe, his son was born. Eventually, both of the Salomon brothers finally settled in the United States. Beginning life in the United States meant that they would have to start anew because everything from the past no longer existed. It is apparent that Bernard and Abram did meet those challenges. The proof is here in this book because of Rick and Joe Salomon, sons of Bernard and Abram respectively, we have the story of their fathers to read today. Each of these stories provides a lesson from history that we can all learn something. Both Rick and Joe continue to keep the legacy of courage and determination alive by passing on their father's story to their children and to others who need to learn important lessons from the past. Their dedication is also evidenced by their active individual commitments to their communities.

The above vignettes are just a sampling of the amazing stories from survivors. There are so many more like them. The four individual stories that were selected for this book were examples of some of the many different kinds of experiences each story tells about. All the stories arise from different circumstances, but ultimately, all those people arrived at the gate of Consul Sugihara. This of course is not the end of their stories. The appendix at the end of this book will update the readers as to what happened to all of the survivors whose stories have been chronicled in this section of this biographical account of Chiune Sugihara. The story of their individual lives and what happened to them after their initial survival offers many more amazing stories that continue today. But each of these stories is an integral part of the story of, Sugihara's Mission of Mercy. It is also an affirmation of the true worth and intrinsic value of Chiune Sugihara's gift of life.

THE DECISION

"I may have disobeyed my government, but I could not disobey my God."

Chiune Sugihara

Chiune had sent his assistants out to calm the crowd. They announced to the crowd that Consul Sugihara would meet with five delegate representatives from the group in order to discuss the situation. It is agreed that Zorach Warhaftig, Samuel Graudenz, Yeoshua Nishri and Zovi Klementenoski were most probably four of the five delegates that first met with Consul Sugihara in his office. There are indications that the fifth delegate could have been a Yosef Orgler or Abram Salomon. What transpired there is debatable because many different versions have been reported. It is clear that Chiune gave each of the representatives an opportunity to present their case as he listened to each one carefully. After listening, he was now more clearly able to understand their dilemma. As he heard about their desperate situation, it became more apparent to him about why the crowd outside his gate had behaved in an impatient and unruly manner. Vice Consul Sugihara first clearly stated his position as Japanese Vice Consul General of Kaunas. He explained that as a representative of his country, Japan, he would have to get permission to issue visas that exceeded his usual quota. Perhaps a dozen or so a day was feasible, but to issue thousands of them would require permission from his Ministry in Tokyo. He also reminded them that he could only issue transit visas that would allow passage through Russia and a stay in Japan for a limited number of days. Those transit visas could only be issued if each of them had an end visa that designated their final destination. He also cautioned them that transit visas could possibly be ineffective if the Soviets would not give them permission to enter their country. He stressed, however, that the primary obstacle would be whether or not he could get permission from his government to issue thousands of Japanese transit visas to Jewish refugees. He informed them that Japan and Germany were on the verge of signing a tripartite pact with Italy. In fact, he stated that it could be happening right at that moment. Therefore, he was very sure that they would never give him permission to do anything that might jeopardize the pending agreement. Despite all the facts that were presented, the representatives pleaded for more consideration and reiterated that if they could not get out of Europe, they faced certain imprisonment and eventually death. Chiune Sugihara was later quoted to have said, "They told me of the horrors they would have to face if captured and I believed them." Consul Sugihara indicated complete understanding of their situation and adjourned the meeting. As they left, he gave his promise that he would continue to give more thought to their problem and would meet with them very soon because he understood the time constraints that both he and the refugees currently faced.

Chiune Sugihara was deeply moved by the refugee's stories. He knew that they were trapped, and if they did not find some avenue of escape, they would end up in German death camps. That first meeting was most likely held sometime around July 24, 1940. Soon after that meeting, he sent a cable dated July 28, 1940, to Foreign Minister Matsuoka. He reported his concerns about recent reports that he had been receiving about "terror activities." He reported that since the Russians began occupying parts of Poland, incidents were reported of seizure of lists of political parties, registries, and illegal arrests that numbered in the thousands. Most of those arrested recently were members of the Polish army and government leaders, leaders of the Socialist and Bundist movements and members of the former ruling class. He described the repressive atmosphere that prevailed. He also reported that he was presently inundated with requests for hundreds of visas daily. The wording of his message strongly indicates his concern and empathy for individual's like Isaac Melamdovich, who was a Bund leader. It is also telling about Chiune's awareness of terrorist activities by the Germans. Here the evidence stands that Chiune believed that the first thing that he must do was to send his report before he sent his request for permission to issue thousands of visas. The family believes that after his meeting with the refugees, he had essentially made up his mind to find some way to help the refugees, but he needed to play for time in order to come up with his plan. Chiune, like Isaac Melandovich, was playing his real life game of chess. As all of these events began to unfold, his memories of what he had witnessed in Manchukuo before he handed in his resignation, flashed before his mind.

Chiune returned to the family living quarters where the members of his family had congregated. From the front windows of the Consulate, a glimpse of the crowd below could be seen behind the closed curtains. Chiune had instructed that the curtains be kept closed because he did not want to excite the crowd below by their appearance. He told his wife, Yukiko, and his sister in law, Setsuko, about what he had learned from his meeting with the delegates. As he told his family the horror stories that were related to him by the refugees, he added that every bit of what they said was also happening all over Europe. The children were very worried and curious about why so many people were standing there. They could feel the tension permeating throughout the room. Hiroki, the eldest was very inquisitive and asked about why there were so many children out there. He later mentioned that after meeting Leo Melamed in Chicago, he wondered if he might have even been one of those children. Hiroki and his younger brother, Chiaki, persisted in asking about those children. Yukiko decided to tell them exactly why they were there. She told them that some very bad people were trying to put them away in prison and that they might even be killed if they did not get away soon. Upon hearing their mother's explanation, they could not believe it. Yukiko reminded young Hiroki about a sign at the park that he had asked about recently. She told him that the sign that they had seen at the park that said, "No Jews Allowed," was about most of those people in front of their home. The children could not

Standing near a gate at the entrance of a park. The sign reads no "Jews Allowed".

comprehend why everything had happened so suddenly. All they could say in response was, "Papa, you must do something to help them." Yukiko assured them that their father was a Japanese samurai and would do what a good samurai would do. Hiroki knew that meant that he would help people in need. Hiroki looked askance at his father as his father affectionately said, "Don't worry, Papa will think of some way to help them."

That night, Chiune's mind was filled with thoughts about what to do and how to help all those people who were still outside waiting and looking for places nearby where they could settle for the night in order to be at the gate early the next morning. Yukiko remembers that he spent a restless night because she heard the sounds made from his bed as he tossed and turned all night. They had discussed the situation together before retiring for the night. Yukiko gave him her assurance that she knew he would make the right choice and that she would stand by his decision. She realized that the safety of his family was his foremost concern. As he restlessly laid in his bed that night, the thoughts that ran through his mind were first his concerns of safety for his family, if he decided to issue the visas. Then he instantly remembered that signing visas would not necessarily help the refugees. He realized that the Soviets would have to agree to allow them to enter Russia and pass through their country. He thought about their

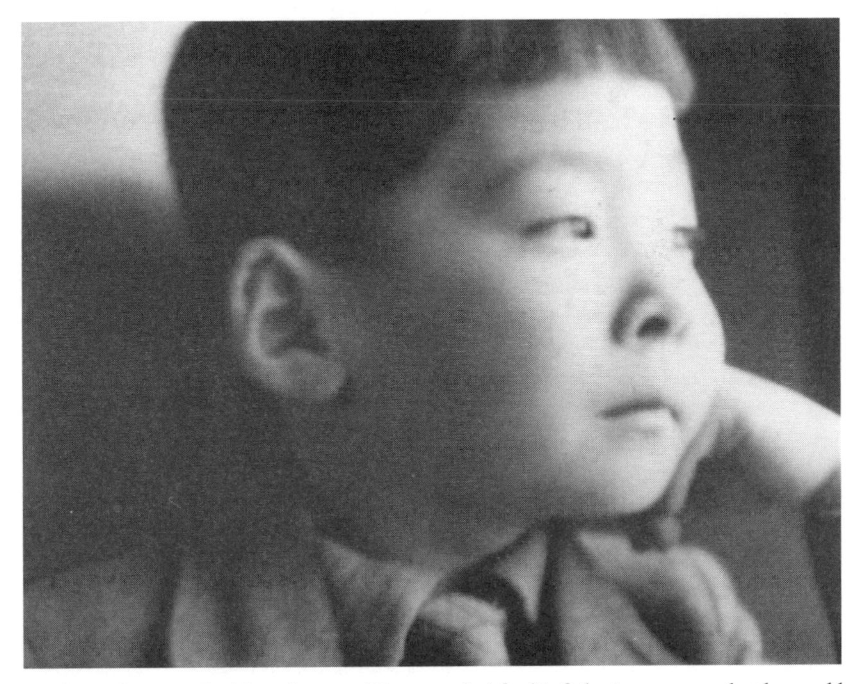

A photo of young Hiroki, at the age of 5 years asked for his father's assurance that he would help the people at the gate and their children.

need for a visa that declared the location of their final destination. The only kind of visa that he could issue to them were transit visas which would serve to get them out of Eastern Europe via Russia and Japan. He worried about the time element. He approximated that the refugees would need at least 50 days to process all their documents and to cross the vast Siberian tundra before they could reach Japan. Even after reaching Japan, they would need weeks to process completion of further documentation. An endless list of problems and concerns churned in his mind. Worst of all, he did not have any viable solutions to any one of the problems that he had thought about. He also couldn't forget the desperate faces of the mothers and their children looking hopefully up to their window. He decided that the first thing to do was to have a meeting with his staff the next day.

The dates are not clear about when Chiune sent his first cable requesting permission to issue visas based on his humanitarian concerns. He also stated strongly in the cable that his request not be denied. Yukiko had the job of handwriting three copies of the cable. The first was sent to the Foreign Minister Matsuoka in Tokyo, the second was sent to the Japanese Ambassador in Riga, Latvia, and the third was sent to Ambassador Oshima of Berlin. The cable sent to the Foreign Ministry in Tokyo would only take one day. In the meantime, Chiune had time to discuss the situation with his staff and it was probably during these meetings that the possibility of using Curacao visas could have originally been discussed. Jan Zwartendijk, Honorary Consul for Dutch Consulate also visited the Japanese Consulate at that time. Yukiko Sugihara notes in her memoir about seeing Jan Zwatendijk visiting the Consulate and attending a meeting. Jan Zwartendijk was an executive for the BP Corporation in Lithuania and was a resident of Kaunas. He had replaced Dr. Tillmans, who was recently dismissed as Consul General when it was discovered that he was a Nazi sympathizer. An interesting fact about this fact is that at the time that Dr. Tillmans was dismissed, Germany had already occupied Holland. In other words, the Dutch Consulate was essentially a Dutch government in a state of exile. That being the case, it helps to understand why the recently appointed Honorary Consul was more likely to be sensitive and sympathetic to the refugee's plight.

The fact that Sugihara was willing to recognize the authority of the Dutch Consulate is another interesting factor. Since Germany had already taken over Holland, and because Japan was an ally of Germany, Sugihara could have refused to recognize Dutch authority in Kaunas. The fact that Sugihara did not do so is very telling about how he regarded the Japan-German alliance. The possibility that Zwartendijk visited the Japanese Consulate for the purpose of discussing the matter of using the Dutch visa is a good one. One of Chiune's Polish intelligence officers, who worked with Sugihara, is to also have declared that Vice Consul Sugihara was involved with the idea from the very start. The contention is that those individuals like Abram Salomon, who became a recipient of one of the first sets of Sugihara-Curacao visas, was able to procure the visas, because they were probably one of the first to hear about the plan. The idea of Sugihara-Curacao visas might have been formulated by the second or third meeting held at the Consulate. In other words, before the announcement was made about the possibility of getting Dutch destination visas, those involved in the original plan, went ahead first to test their idea. After the plan was set in motion, and the individuals successfully got both of their visas, word got around about this scheme and hundreds of people began to come to the Japanese Consulate from July 27, 1940. They were all frantic in hopes of acquiring something that would give them a last chance for escape.

It is important here to explain the significance of the Dutch visa. The exact sequence of events about how the plan developed, will never be determined. What is important is that there were individuals who were willing to be participants towards making this "bogus" document possible. Each of the participants had a choice of either refusing or getting involved in this "charade." Those who chose to become involved created the chance for thousands to escape capture. It is not clear if there was any connection between the following three individuals and Vice Consul Sugihara, but the fact is that three Dutch nationals originally made inquiry to Zwartendijk about issuing those Dutch passports that stated no visa necessary for Curacao-Surinam. The three Dutch nationals were Nathan Gutwirth, and his siblings Rachel and Levi Sternheim. They also recognized that on those passports was an added statement that required that the recipients acquire approval from the governor of those small Dutch West Indies Islands. The outrageous suggestion was proposed that, what if the last sentence concerning the governor's approval were deleted, would it not solve the problem of acquiring an end visa.

Zwartendijk made an inquiry to L. P. De Decker, the Dutch Ambassador to Latvia. In a word, he miraculously agreed by saying, "Yes." His only request was that it be written in French. Jan Zwartendijk immediately set to work with help from volunteers. One of those volunteers was George Liebert, whose story was told about how helpful and useful his knowledge of French became. As a result, Sugihara and Zwartendijk churned out thousands of their visas. Whereas, the Dutch Consul received approval from his superior, Sugihara made a decision to defy authority and to do so based on his own humanitarian principals. He thereby chose to risk his life and career in order to save lives. Many of the recipients of the Sugihara visa did in fact not have a Curacao visa to go along with their Sugihara visa. However, by their own good fortune, they also were able to reach the shores of Japan safely. According to accounts given by the refugees, many of them interestingly remembered that while the Japanese visas cost a mere 2 Lithuanian litas; the Dutch visas had costs them about 11 litas.

In the meantime, Sugihara continued sending cables asking specifically for permission to issue visas. The five representatives visited the Consulate several times a day to inquire about their status. His replies from Tokyo only reiterated the established requirement that a final destination be established with a guarantor willing to be their sponsor should all be in place. Polish citizenship was another requirement. Most of the people outside of his gate did not have one or all of the required documents. By now, Sugihara realized that there was a possibility to provide a visa stating a final destination by using the Curacao "bogus" visa. But he realized that he had many other issues that he needed to address. He was concerned about the safety of his family so he gathered them together to discuss the matter of their safety. He informed his wife that he had decided to go ahead with plans to help the refugees. He told his wife and Setsuko that there was a window of opportunity to return to Japan if they left immediately. He explained that he did not want to jeopardize their safety because of what he was about to do. Yukiko was relieved to hear about her husband's decision and said that she was determined to stay by his side and wanted to help in any way that she could. Setsuko and the children did not want to be separated from the family and return to Japan alone. It was finally decided that they would stay together. Chiune agreed to let them stay under certain conditions. He requested that Yukiko promise that she and any other member of the family stay completely out of view and not participate in any activities connected with the issuing of visas. His instructions were that the family was to stay away from all business connected with helping the refugees. He explained that he was giving these instructions to protect them. The reason being that in case he was ever accused and punished for issuing visas, he would be able to truthfully declare that the family was not involved in any way. Yukiko promised, but assured Chiune of her complete support and encouragement. Chiune always cherished the fact that his wife supported him and that she was in complete agreement with him about their decision that it was the only right thing to do.

Chiune felt that he now had certain things under control. First, he had discussed with the family, his concern for their safety and had received the assurance of his wife's complete support. The other obstacle concerning the need for an end visa was being addressed. He continued cabling the Foreign Ministry for approval to issue hundreds of visas, but did not have much hope of receiving it. Thus, he continued to forge ahead with his own plans that would insure that the transit visas that he was planning to issue could be effectively utilized. What would be the point of issuing visas that would not help anyone? The next obstacle was to extend his stay in Kaunas. He would not be able to issue very many visas if he were to leave on the date that he was ordered to leave. In fact, he had just been recently reminded of his orders to vacate his office by both the Russian and Japanese authorities. The next important concern on his list was that he also needed to somehow obtain permission or get some indication from the Russians that they would allow recipients of his visa to go across Russia. Chiune decided that he did not have a moment to wait, a visit to the Soviet Consulate was now in order.

Vice Consul Sugihara was confident about conferring with Russians. He remembered his days in Manchukuo and his life with his first White Russian wife. He understood the Russians and he spoke the language like a native. Besides, he had gotten to know the Russian Consul quite well and they had gradually come to enjoy having occasional drinks together while exchanging amusing stories. His interview with the Consul began informally and he was greeted warmly by him. Vodka was served. They enjoyed exchanging information and talked about their personal lives as they continued drinking and conversing. Earlier in the story, it was mentioned that Chiune had an unusually strong constitution and that drinking large quantities of alcohol did not affect him; this ability served him well on this day. When he felt that the Russian Consul was relaxed and in a convivial mood, Sugihara broached the subject of the Jewish refugees. He proposed his idea that if they were able to get permission to cross Siberia on his transit visas, it would help to generate funds for the government run Trans Siberian Railway. The Russian Consul was well aware that through the American Joint Distribution Committee, and other funding groups in the United States, they would be well assured of receiving the funds for their tickets. The Consul agreed that selling tickets to the refugees would definitely increase their revenue. Chiune then addressed the fact that in order to assure that thousands of tickets could be sold, it would only be possible if he were given an extension to stay longer. The Russian Consul agreed to give him an extension of 30 more days to implement all of the proposed ideas. Vice Consul Sugihara left the Consulate with a great sense of relief and was exhilarated because he had successfully accomplished his goals for that day.

Before he made the official announcement that he would be issuing visas, he met with his staff member, Gudje. Chiune was aware of Gudje's connection with Berlin and told him of his plans to help the refugees. He advised Gudje to leave the Consulate so that he would not be implicated with him about helping the Jews and perhaps receive severe punishment for participating. Instead of accepting the offer to leave, Gudje asked him if he could stay because he wanted to help him. Chiune was touched by his offer and allowed him to stay. Moshe Zupnik, is a survivor who is in his nineties. He is presently living in Brooklyn. He was a representative of the Mir Yeshiva group. He remembered working alongside Gudje. Zupnik had come into the office requesting visas for all the students and teachers of the Mir Yeshiva, a rabbinical institution of learning. He assured Chiune that they would be receiving funding from a benefactor in the United States. Zupnik had apparently heard about the Curacao visas and assured Chiune that all the students and teachers of the Yeshiva had already received them. Chiune agreed to help them. However, when it was discovered that there were about 300 visas that needed to be processed for the entire school, Chiune was stunned. He asked Gudje to work on the visas for that group. Zupnik realized that it was a big job for one person to tackle by himself, so he volunteered to help him. Gudje asked Chiune for his approval to allow Zupnik to help him. Chiune looked at Zupnik, and said, "Go ahead, you can help him." Zupnik remembers Gudje well and describes him as a fine man that once said to him, "Remember, life is like a wheel. At one time you're on the top, but eventually, you'll get to the bottom. Don't forget that." Those words of Gudje proved to be prophetic. It was later reported that he had been killed while serving in the German army soon

Gudje with Hiroki, left, and Chiaki. Gudje, who was sent from Berlin to keep an eye on the Kaunas office, was a favorite of the children. He taught Hiroki how to speak German.

after he had left Kaunas. Hiroki also had kind remembrances of the man who had played with him and his brothers and had taught him how to speak German. As a result of the collaboration of Gudje, Moshe Zupnick and Sugihara, the entire Mir Yeshiva of more than 300 students and teachers were saved. Today, their centers of learning are in New York and Israel. It is a great tribute to Chiune Sugihara that because of his life saving deed, the entire rabbinical teachings of the Talmud were saved for the generations to come. All of the important elements were now in place to enable Chiune to begin issuing visas. He had been continuing to issue visas each day to people who met all the set requirements, but now, he felt that the stage was set to begin his humanitarian intervention on a grander scale. He was ready to announce his decision to issue visas to everyone that he possibly could. The Sugihara Family will never forget the scene below their window when the announcement was made that the Japanese Vice Consul would issue visas to as many people as would be possible before he was to close his office. As a result of his announcement, there were shouts of jubilation, people were hugging each other, as tears of joy poured down their faces. The scene below brought smiles and even tears to the eyes of the Sugihara family as they watched the crowd rejoicing. They watched the father's joyously raising their children up for the Sugihara family to see. A system of handing out numbers to the refugees was developed. This was to insure orderly conduct and efficiency. It was first believed that each individual stood in line to get their individual visas, but according to George Liebert who was actually there, that was not how it worked. According to

George, people were instructed to hand in documents in an orderly way and then they were brought into the Consulate in bunches. When Sugihara completed each bunch, they were handed back to the waiting individuals at the gate. Then the next group or groups of numbered individuals were called in proper order to have their visas stamped and signed. At first, Chiune followed all the protocol that was required when he officially issued visas and kept a judicious account of his list. When Chiune noticed that the lines of people continued to grow, he decided that he must speed up the process. In doing so, his records were no longer accurate. He only had a couple of weeks before he was to vacate his office. Since he was the only one who had the authority to issue the visa, he realized that the task that he had committed himself to do was a monumental one. He had a goal of trying to complete between 200-300 visas a day. Yukiko applied salves on his arms and massaged them every night. The stamina and endurance he had developed as a young man in Gifu and Nagoya was now tested and it enabled him to continue the task for over twenty days. By now, he had received specific instructions from Foreign Minister Matsuoka, to NOT issue visas due to concerns of public safety and because the shipping companies could not insure the safety of the passengers. Chiune realized that he was officially defying his government's orders and he was prepared to face the consequences.

TRANSIT VISA.

Seen for the journey through Japen (to Suranam, Curaçao and other Netherlands' colonies.) 1940 VIII. 9

Consul du Japon à Kaunas.

CONSULAT DU JAPON KAUNAS LITHUANIE

Wixy-Visas

The Sugihara / Curacao Visa

As the day for closing the Consulate approached, he continued churning out visa after visa. The family had finally packed all their goods. Chiune destroyed all official records and information that he could not take along with him. He thanked the staff for their support and promised that if he were ever arrested, they had his assurance that he would not implicate anyone who was involved in helping him issue the visas. He had Borislav make the announcement that they would be staying at the Hotel Metropolis in Kaunas Town before boarding their train for Berlin. The stay in the hotel was for the purpose of giving Chiune a chance to rest before heading for Berlin. He had officially issued 2139 visas on a list that ended on August 24, 1940. Official numbers did not mean anything to him. At this point, he was completely committed and dedicated to saving as many lives as possible. In the end, he issued visas to anyone who had some kind of document that he could stamp his official seal on. There were later reports about a stamp making shop that copied his stamp and produced an acceptable likeness. These stamps did indeed serve its purpose because several people were reported to have escaped using the counterfeit stamps. His Polish intelligence officers related that some stamps were produced with dates that were backdated. Those forged stamps made it possible to make it appear that Chiune had issued those visas while he was still in Kaunas. Joseph Shimpkin, a worker for the Joint Distribution, also recalls using forged stamps. Joseph Shimpkin later became a family friend of the Sugihara family. People continued coming in droves, desperate to get their visas. Chiune did not get his needed rest because he could not refuse the people who continued coming to the hotel. He continued issuing visas in the hotel and at the train station before boarding the train for Berlin. The exact amount of visas issued by Chiune Sugihara can never be accurately estimated. Adding to the confusion, is the fact that the forged ones, amazingly, did save lives as well. Nevertheless, today there are thousand of survivors and their descendants that can attest to the fact that the visas, forged or authentic, were truly precious live saving visas.

THE AFTERMATH

"If you believe in fate, believe in it, for your own good."
Ralph Waldo Emerson

After weeks of relentlessly issuing visa after visa, with just short periods of rest, Chiune was exhausted. As soon as the train started moving and heading for Berlin, Chiune instantly fell asleep into much needed deep sleep. But just before the train was about to depart, he looked out of his window and saw the desperate people continuing to beg for visas. He was filled with sadness as he saw their desperate eyes and shouted to them, "Please forgive me, I can no longer help you." However, before he boarded the train, he did leave some instructions to those left behind. He urged people who did not get his visa to try to get to Moscow where he thought it would be possible to get a visa. Chiune apparently had some reason to believe that someone in the Japanese Legation in Moscow would be helpful to them by trying to get transit visas for them to go to Japan.

As soon as they arrived in Berlin, they went to report to Ambassador Saburo Kurusu. He had just recently temporarily replaced Ambassador Oshima. Ambassador Hiroshi Oshima had just been ordered back to Tokyo. Unlike his predecessor, Oshima, Ambassador Kurusu was considered to be pro-United States and Pro-Great Britain. Kurusu did not bring up nor did he indicate any knowledge of what was eventually to be referred to as the "Incident in Lithuania." He was very friendly and chose to tell the Sugiharas about the latest tragedy that had just occurred at the Berlin zoo. Apparently, after one of the air raid attacks, the elephants at the zoo escaped from their confines because it had been bombed during the air raid. Unconfined elephants posed a threat to the community, so unfortunately, they had to be killed.

While Chiune was feverishly issuing visas, Europe was undergoing great turmoil. It seemed that since there was so much going on all over Europe, the "Incident" was overlooked. Even before Chiune began his "Mission of Mercy," the Soviets had defeated Finland in March of 1940. Hitler had successfully invaded and conquered Denmark and Norway. In April, they invaded Greece. Great Britain was engaged in battles in the Atlantic. By September, a few weeks before Chiune was issuing his visas, Germany had begun air raids over England.

(left) Picture of Aunt Setsuko and the Sugihara children peering out of the window of their train before leaving Kaunas, Lithuania. (right) After signing thousands of visas, the family reported back to Berlin in 1940. The family stands before the Brandenberg Gate in Berlin.

Hitler's Final Solution, his mission to drive all Jews out of Europe, was in full force. Over 400,000 Polish Jews were rounded up and herded into the Warsaw Ghettoes. As the war escalated, crises after crises mounted all over Europe. Under these horrific circumstances, it was understandable that what was happening in Kaunas could have been overlooked. Another factor that may have affected why what happened in Lithuania was not given noticeable attention could have been because of the prevailing instability of the Japanese government. It was the army that appointed Chiune to the Consulate position in Kaunas. By 1939, the army was essentially controlling the government and the Foreign Ministry. It was a known fact that Chiune advocated for peaceful diplomatic measures to solve differences. He believed that the utilization of all possible diplomatic measures towards finding solutions for problems should be the priority of the government. It was known that he was pro-peace. Since it was the army that was responsible for his appointment to the Kaunas position, they may have felt reluctant to reprimand him. The family believed that repercussions from what happened in Kaunas could be delayed. In fact they hoped that it would be forgotten. Since they did not receive any signs or warnings of upcoming reprimand, it appeared to the Sugiharas that perhaps the authorities decided that it would be more prudent to withhold reprimanding Chiune until a later time. They believed that the army may have just decided to allow him to serve the government while his skills were still needed by them. Interestingly, when Chiune did attempt to tell Ambassador Kurusu about the incident in Lithuania, he pointedly chose to ignore him, and instead continued his discussion with him about his new assignment.

After his official meeting with Kurusu, Chiune returned home and cheerfully informed Yukiko that there was no discussion about what happened in Lithuania. He proudly reported to her about his new assignment as Consul General in Prague, Czechoslovakia. His new orders were to replace Consul General Ichige. Another point of interest is that it was Foreign Minister Matsuoka who had decided to give him this new assignment. He was the person that had recently ordered Chiune not to issue the visas. Several years ago Foreign Minister Yosuke Matsuoka, was the person that lead Japan's secession from the League of Nations. When the League voted for sanctions against Japan in favor of China, the Japanese representatives defiantly walked out denouncing their membership in the League. In another incident, Matsuoka was also to have answered Foreign Minister Joachim von Ribbentrop, by saying to him, "We may have concluded a treaty with you, but we never promised to be an Anti-Semite." This was his answer when Ribbentrop had requested that Japan return all of the Jewish refugees that were under Japanese protective custody in Shanghai. Shanghai was then a territory of Japan and the refugees were living there in safety. Many of them were recipients of Sugihara's visas. Matsuoka's refusal clarified Japan's position and their stand on racial issues. Was Foreign Minister Matsuoka aware of what Chiune had done in Kaunas, Lithuania and preferred not to acknowledge it, or was it because he did not yet know about the "incident?" It is strongly possible that he did not know because Sugihara had delayed sending out his report and visa list about what occurred in Kaunas to the Foreign Ministry in Tokyo. The reason for the delay was because he hoped to allow time for the refugees to arrive safely in Japan before the authorities would be notified and made aware of the fact that thousands of refugees could soon be landing. Sugihara's apprehensions were due to the fact that he thought that, if the authorities knew about the refugee's arrival beforehand, they might be stopped before they could arrive in Japan. Although all of these issues were on Chiune's mind, the Sugihara family was elated to hear the news of Chiune's new appointment, despite the fact that they were told that it would be a temporary one. When the assignment was given, he had been warned that Germany had recently ordered that all Consulates in Czechoslovakia would soon be closed.

PRAGUE

As the Sugihara family was getting settled in Prague, the Triple Alliance between Japan, Germany, and Italy had finally concluded in September 27, 1940. Germany relentlessly continued her drive to conquer Europe. In rapid succession, Bulgaria, Czechoslovakia, Hungary, and Romania had also joined the Alliance. Life in Prague was reminiscent of their life in Helsinki. They hosted and attended dinner parties, theater openings, and all different kinds of official functions. The Consulate was a magnificent two-story structure that faced the Moldau River. The interior was decorated in the Rococo style with draped silk wall hangings, Czechoslovakian crystal chandeliers, and rooms of gold and silver. One could hear the bells of the St. Svatyvit Cathedral chiming daily, each morning and evening, as the sounds resounded through the medieval streets. They had a much larger household staff than they had in Kaunas. The staff included nine members. There were five maids, one cook, and three officers. During his short stay in Prague, Chiune was able to issue 69 more visas to Jews who came to his office. Chiune continued to keep his word about helping as many people as he could.

During their Prague assignment, there was one incident that involved Foreign Minister Ribbentrop. The Sugiharas were not admirers of the German Foreign Minister because they were aware of his part in what happened in Lithuania. When the German-Soviet Non-Aggression Pact was concluded, Ribbentrop had secretly signed an agreement to divide Poland with the Soviets, and the plan was to eventually annex Lithuania. That agreement was the cause for the sudden and desperate efforts of the Jewish refugees to find a way to escape out of Europe. The incident involving Chiune and Ribbentrop happened during a special meeting that Ribbentrop had called for so that he could make an announcement to all the Diplomats assigned to posts in Czechoslovakia. As the delegates arrived, he sat arrogantly behind his desk, under a huge portrait of Hitler. Then he roared out his new decree ordering that all diplomats were to leave their posts immediately. This announcement was not an unexpected one because Chiune had been previously told that his assignment in Prague would most likely be a temporary one. However, the arrogant manner that Ribbentrop delivered the order was quite intimidating. The fact that he had a very large ferocious looking German Shepherd, dutifully guarding the entrance of the hall where the diplomats had congregated, added to the already oppressive atmosphere. Germany's recent conquests further fueled Ribbentrop's arrogance. No one attending that meeting seemed to dare to question his authority. As the Diplomats listened quietly, the silence was suddenly broken by Chiune's voice. In a clear and confident tone, he questioned the Foreign Minister's order. As he spoke up, he emphasized that he was speaking as a representative of his country, Japan. He pointedly reminded Ribbentrop that Japan was an equal partner in their alliance with Germany. As an equal partner he demanded that an explanation be given for the sudden orders that had just given to the assembled group. Whatever Ribbentrop's answer was, Chiune succeeded in informing the German Foreign Minister that Japan would not accept being treated like a subordinate. As equal partners, they expected to be treated and addressed respectfully. This was another incident that revealed Chiune's tendency to have the courage to stand up against the kind of unjustified authority that Ribbentrop represented. For Ribbentrop, it was an incident that he was unlikely to forget very soon. The assignment in the Prague Consulate lasted for six months. During that period, Chiune began to write up his report about the Incident in Lithuania. Orders had been sent to all diplomats to send in reports listing the number of visas that had been issued. Chiune hoped that the refugees who received his stamped visas would have already safely crossed the Japan Sea to Japan before officials became aware of what was happening. Very soon after the orders were given to vacate the Prague Consulate, Ambassador Oshima had returned to his post in Berlin. He requested that Chiune report to him when he returned to Berlin. Ambassador Kurusu had left Berlin in order to prepare for his new assignment as special envoy to the United States. Oshima had new orders for Chiune. He told him that it would be necessary to open up a new Consulate in Koenigsberg, Germany. He continued to explain that since Koenigsberg was near the Russian border, it was suitable to give the assignment to someone fluent in Russian. Chiune was allowed to have a staff of a few officers to go along with him. It was clear to Chiune that his primary mission would again be to collect intelligence.

Meanwhile, Germany's planned invasion into Russia was delayed by their invasions into the smaller countries of Europe. This delay eventually proved to be fatal to Germany's drive to take over Europe. By now the refugees that had received Sugihara visas had endured many hardships getting through Siberia and eluding capture by Russian authorities and soldiers. Some of them slowly began arriving at Tsuruga Port in late October of 1940. Approximately 25 refugees with Sugihara visas were the first to arrive safely to Japan.

KOENIGSBERG

The Sugihara family moved to Koenigsberg in March of 1941. They rented a large two-story house as their home and it also served as a Consulate. There was press coverage in the Koenigsberg newspapers about Chiune's and his family's arrival. The children liked their new home with its large garden. They especially loved playing with the tame squirrels that lived in their new backyard. The squirrels were not afraid to climb on the children's shoulders and to eat peanuts that were handed to them. It was a quiet town and they had a good quiet life. The air raids had not yet begun there. They still had some social functions to attend, but they were usually small dinner parties. One memorable official function that the family held a few days after their arrival was, Koinobori no Hi (Children's Day). People from the community learned about Japanese Children's Day, and how it was celebrated. The German children learned that children in Japan made carps (koi) shaped kites and flew it from the rooftops of their homes. The carp had a symbolic meaning that denoted courage, perseverance, and tenacity. Children in Japan were encouraged to develop those traits. Following the kite flying ceremony, they were invited to a party in the Consulate where they were served Japanese cakes.

Meanwhile, as Chiune was feverishly working on his intelligence reports, the Germans were escalating their war activities and reaching out in all directions throughout Europe. It was obvious that something important was going to happen soon. Chiune had to follow up on the recent rash of reports that had been received and was busy confirming them. He reported that there were unusual increases in troop movements. For example, very recently, at least ten Nazi army trains have been arriving from Berlin daily. A 30,000 ton ship and ten steamships were moored at Pilau Port; and in Prussia, a large concentration of German soldiers had suddenly arrived. On a road in Lithuania that was actually the border between Germany and Russia, German tanks were observed to be mobilizing. Tensions increased as the Soviets tanks were moving in to protect their border. Soviet observation towers appeared overnight and grain in great quantities were being shipped to the area.

Tensions were high everywhere. It was now ordered that all Jews were to wear yellow stars and curfew laws were enforced. As Chiune personally witnessed what was happening to the large remaining Jewish population, he hoped that the refugees that had received his visas had safely escaped. This was the beginning of martial law. Chiune experienced the same sense of despair that he had when Japan came under martial law that 2.26 day. He also recalled having the same sense of foreboding when the Japanese army had literally taken over the country during his post in Manchukuo. The Germans were also probably quite disturbed when it was learned that Japanese Foreign Minister Matsuoka had gone to Russia to meet with Joseph Stalin. Having received intelligence reports from Chiune Sugihara and others operatives that Germany was about to invade the Soviet Union,

(top) Photo taken in Koenigsberg for the celebration of Japanese Children's Day (bottom) Chiune and Yukiko are pictured having a discussion with a German officer. Collaborationg with members of the German army was one of his duties. Circa 1940–41.

he agreed to sign a pact with Russian premier, Stalin. The pact guaranteed that Japan would refrain from going against the Soviets in any acts of aggression. The Anti-Comintern Pact was signed on April 13, 1941. This act affirmed that Japan's alliance with Germany was indeed a "Hollow Alliance."

Germany continued her relentless assaults, and during the summer of 1941, had invaded the stretch of land from Finland to Romania. The German army was experiencing a sense of superiority as a result of their recent victories. They did not expect nor were they prepared for what awaited them as they started their invasion of Russia. Hitler had not learned a lesson from history. Napoleon Bonaparte of France had in the past, also started his invasion of Russia late in the summer, and was ultimately defeated because they could not defeat the Russians in their unforgivable and treacherous land of ice and snow. Tragically, history was going to repeat itself again.

For the Japanese people, December 7, 1941, as President Roosevelt appropriately coined it, was indeed, "A Day of Infamy." For Chiune, it was the beginning of the end. He had hoped that this day would never arrive, but feared that it was inevitable. He had hoped that his beloved country, Japan, would take the road of peace and to avoid war at all costs. His mentor, Hirota, Koki had always maintained that the only reason for the existence of an army was for the sake of self-defense. When he heard of the news of the attack on Pearl Harbor, he experienced feelings of emptiness, sadness, and despair. He was saddened that his countrymen allowed themselves to be led blindly by militarists. He felt emptiness as he realized that many lives would be lost fighting a meaningless war. He was in despair as he thought about his beautiful homeland and the tragic disasters that would fall upon his country and its people. He felt helpless because he could not do anything to stop the fanatic nationalism that had overtaken his country. This nationalism was what had further fueled the army's power to take over the government. Just as the Germans were reveling in their small victories, Japan was also experiencing the same phenomena in the regions of the Pacific Islands.

Tragically, both Germany and Japan were driven by their fanatic and overzealous sense of superiority. Chiune felt that the only ray of hope lay in the fact that his country and her people would someday have the chance to learn a lesson from this mistake and get a second chance to be a great country whose citizens valued dignity and respect for human life. In the meantime, he understood that he must not abandon his country and its people because there were many others in his country that felt as he did. He realized that he must continue to serve in the best way he could until this tragic turn of events would end as soon as possible. He understood that as a representative and servant of Japan and her people, he must continue to serve in a way that best represented them. He also remembered that when he and Yukiko had decided to take the risk and made their decision to issue visas against orders, they did believe that they were serving in the best interest of their country. He vowed not to lose hope for his country and her people and to continue serving them as best as he could. He recalled the motto of his former school, Waseda University. The meaning of the motto was essentially that one's highest reward in life was to serve the people; and in order to serve the people well, one must listen to the voice of the people. Chiune believed in his heart that when he had issued those visas, he was listening to the voice of the people. He hoped that he had represented the true heart of the people of Japan when he chose to participate in saving lives rather than destroying lives.

Life in the once peaceful town of Koenigsberg changed overnight. Although Yukiko, Setsuko and her children were given an opportunity to return to Japan before conditions worsened, they again opted to stay and endure the rest of the war together with Chiune. Many activities were prohibited such as dancing in public. Air raids over major cities by the British came regularly. The Germans continued instituting insidious acts epitomized by the announcement of their Final Solution, the plan for the extermination of all Jews. The Sugihara family continued activities required of diplomats. For example, they dutifully participated in a ceremony where they marched with German soldiers to the grave of General Paul von Hindenburg. The children had opportunities to enjoy swimming in the Baltic Sea. Chiune realized that closure of his Consulate was imminent. He knew that he was under heavy surveillance by the Germans. He believed that they were very aware of his intelligence work. At times he even thought that perhaps they had already discovered about what he had done in Kaunas. Assuming that they were keeping intense scrutiny of his movements, he guessed that they were aware of the fact that he still continued to collaborate with his Polish operatives. Word was out that the Germans no longer wanted him in Koenigsberg. Even today, there are dossiers in the government archives in Berlin indicating that surveillance had been made of Sugihara's movements. As expected, he was told that he was reassigned to a new post.

Chiune Sugihara is pictured between two German Officers while on their way to attend a ceremony for General Paul Hindenburg at his grave site.

BUCHAREST

His next posting was in the Japanese Legation of Bucharest, Rumania. At the time of his appointment, he was given the position of minister. However, because the former minister was unable to leave for Japan due to the escalation of war activities, Chiune became the resident Russian translator. The former minister in fact became his superior there. His name was Minister Tsutsui. Tsutsui was reputed to be notoriously pro-German and very anti-Semitic. Under his supervision, Chiune's activities were very restricted and he was always under strict supervision. Even if he were able be more independent, there was not much he could have done. By June of 1941, the Germans had essentially rounded up every Jewish person and the Holocaust was set on a full course of murder and destruction. While their stay in Bucharest lasted for about two years, the Sugihara's experienced what it was like living under the cloud of war.

While the war raged on in Europe and in the Pacific, the Sugihara family's life was relatively quiet for a short while. Chiune had more time to spend with family. It seemed to them that they were far removed and untouched by the war and its effects. In the summer there was an abundance of fresh fruits to eat. Wine was plentiful made from all the varied fruits that were grown there. They enjoyed their Sunday drives appreciating the beautiful scenes of the countryside. In the winter the children played in the snow and enjoyed making the unique style of snowmen that the children made there. Instead of making round parts for bodies, they made figures with arms and legs protruding from their square shaped bodies.

The tide of the war was changing and Germany's defeat became more imminent. Bombings by the Allies continued and increased. It became necessary to build bomb shelters. Since Chiune was the only officer in the Legation with a family of children, it was suggested that the family move to a country house in an area that would be a lesser target for bombing raids. Concern for the welfare of the children prompted the Sugiharas to move immediately to Poiana Brasov. It was a cottage on a hill near the town of Brasov. Before leaving for Brasov, over half of Bucharest had already been destroyed. On their way to Brasov, they perilously escaped with their lives when the Germans set up smoke screens. Since they couldn't see where they were going, they maneuvered their car between smoke screens, while at the same time, praying for their lives. The purpose for setting up the screens was to prevent the detection of German oil fields by the Allies. Miraculously, the family was able to reach the safety of their cottage among the isolated hills near the town of Brasov.

During their stay in Rumania, Chiune experienced one of the most worrisome events in his life that involved Yukiko. Chiune had warned Yukiko that it was very likely that they would be leaving Rumania very soon because it was expected that the Soviets would be attacking the country very soon. Concerned about some articles that she considered to be personally very precious, she made the decision to

A photo taken at Poiana Brasou in Rumania. They moved to the country house in order to avoid the bomb attacks going on in Bucharest.

go quickly back to Rumania to retrieve some of her goods that she had left in the Consulate. One particular item that she did not want to lose was her autographed photo of Finnish composer, Sibelius. On the way, her car broke down. A German soldier offered to take her onto Bucharest. On the way, they encountered another German soldier walking along the road who informed them that it would be impossible to go to Bucharest. He told them that the whole German army was in retreat and trying to get to the border through the forests. Yukiko had no alternative but to go with them to the forests where the soldiers were in hiding. They were all trying to reach borders where they might find a safe route to safety. Rumanian soldiers who had joined with the Soviets against the German forces had the German army trapped in the forest. Yukiko found herself right in the middle of this melee. In her own words, she described it as, "It was just like being in a movie." After experiencing unforgettable scenes of shootings and the death of a German soldier who helped to save her life, she miraculously survived the ordeal. After eight days of harrowing experiences that followed one dangerous situation after another, it ended with her being captured by Rumanian partisans. After intensive interrogation, she was finally returned to her cottage in Poiana Brasov.

The minute Yukiko saw Chiune, she noticed that he had lost a considerable amount of weight. She was distraught to realize all the pain and worry she had caused because of her foolish desire to get her treasured memento. Of course she was overjoyed to be greeted by the happy and joyous greetings of her children who were led to believe that she had been away because she was attending some diplomatic function. Chiune had been out every sleepless day and night, looking for her. He had contacted every possible source to find out if there was any word of her. During his search, he himself encountered danger such as Russian soldiers pointing their guns at him. Because of his Russian language ability, he was finally able to convince them that he was not a spy. In fact, he was even able to get their cooperation in helping him to locate his missing wife.

Hitler committed suicide in April of 1945. Germany's defeat was inevitable. The world awaited Japan's surrender. There was no word from Ambassador Oshima in Berlin. Instructions of what to do were not forth coming. Chiune decided that it was time to return to Bucharest. Finally warnings were received that they should expect Soviet soldiers to eventually come to take them away. The family had packed and they were ready to go in the event that they would soon be coming to take them away. Finally, that day did come and they were confined to a military officer's residence. Along with them were other Japanese families who were members of the Military Attache'. They lived under restricted conditions and were not free to go outside the confines of their residence. There was no word from Ambassador Oshima. As Chiune had feared, the Soviets declared war against Japan on August 9, 1945. That sped up Japan's decision to end the war by their signing the Potsdam Declaration on August 15, 1945. It was six days after the Soviets declared war on Japan. These circumstances did not bode well for the Sugihara family because they were under Soviet military arrest. Now there existed the threat that they could be sent to Siberia. They were especially concerned because of Chiune's status as persona non grata in Russia. Several days after Japan's surrender, Soviet soldiers came to the residence asking to speak with Chiune. The family waited nervously expecting to hear the worst. After a brief discussion, Chiune came out of the meeting and informed his family and the other Japanese families that they would be placed in an internment camp somewhere in the outskirts of Bucharest. They were loaded into a truck along with all of the belongings that they were able to take with them and headed for a life unlike, and very different from the one they had been previously living for the past eight years. It was as Gudje had said before he left Kauna, "Life is like a wheel, one day you are up, and the next day you are down."

PRISONERS OF WAR

"Under a government which imprisons unjustly, the true place for a just man is also a prison."
Henry David Thoreau

In the fall of 1945, they became prisoners of war and were placed in camps referred to as internment camps. Their captors were soldiers of the Russian army. They were assigned to a section that consisted of other Japanese families connected with the diplomatic corps and with members of the military attache'. German soldiers were also placed in the camp in another section. Their living conditions and treatment were much harsher than that experienced by the Sugihara family. Instead of their feather blankets, they now slept on straw. They were constantly trying to warm up because their only source of heat was a small coal stove placed in the center of one of their two rooms. The children were adaptable, but they were deprived of nutritious food. Their basic diet was primarily some kind of diluted meat soup and dark bread and garlic. On occasion they were able to secretly obtain fresh fruits from a nearby farmer. The two main issues that caused the biggest concern for them were sleep deprivation and their state of uncertainty. It was difficult to sleep when one could not get warmed up, and the straw bedding was something that was difficult to become adjusted to. However, their foremost concern was the daily uncertainty of their life. Yukiko was always in fear of the fact that someone would recognize Chiune as an enemy of the Soviets and send him off to Siberia. There were always rumors of soldiers that suddenly disappeared and were never seen again. Most of the prisoners assumed that those who disappeared were sent to Siberian prison camps. There were some pleasurable moments that broke the bleakness of their environment. For example, Hiroki remembered being entertained by a group of German soldiers who gave a musical concert. He recalls that they were very entertaining as they robustly sang songs and were accompanied by a violin and piano.

They were there for less than a year when they were told that they had permission to leave. They were loaded on a freight train that was essentially a cargo train with all the belongings that they were able to take with them. They were not going to escape from the cold because by fall, the normal temperature there was about -45 degrees. The train had the same kind of heating system that again consisted of a small coal stove. The family could usually be found hovering over that little stove. Fortunately for them, the children were strong and did not become seriously ill; although there was concern for Kurichan, who had always been the most frail of the three boys. The fact that there were no bathing facilities was especially disturbing to Yukiko and her sister Setsuko. They all had to endure feeling very unclean day after day. But perhaps the very worst part of their travel on the train was the presence of fleas and lice. Their train, actually being a cargo train, carried livestock that were covered with all of those insects. Chiune felt saddened as he observed his children suffering intense itchiness from their bites. As winter approached, the cold became more intense. Whenever they had to step outside to go to toilets or just go outside to relieve their bladders, the urine virtually froze before their eyes. When their eyelashes became frozen, it was very painful. They were very fortunate because no one had frostbite. Everyone learned very quickly not to touch metal objects because the area that was touched would instantly stick and the effects of the burn were very painful. At each stop when they had to go through inspections, they noticed that their baggage was getting less and less because it seemed that something was stolen during each inspection. They finally stopped in Odessa, and were told that they would be there for a few days. During their long trek across Siberia, Chiune had ample opportunity to reminisce. Riding on the slow train heading for the east, he probably recalled the trains that had passed by his home in Nagoya when he was a young man. He probably recalled that sad day when he boarded the train to leave for Tokyo as he waved good bye to his mother and brothers. His life was full of experiences that related to trains. How many times did he ride across the vast plains of Manchuria on a train? He cherished one of the most exciting times of his life when he crossed the United States from the west coast to the east coast by train. He could not forget how proud he felt when he was told that he would be in charge of the purchase of the Northern Manchurian Railroad as the secretary for the Purchasing department. Anywhere he went in Japan, travel was primarily by train. It was also train tickets that he was helping those Jewish refugees to get so that they would have a chance to escape. He nostalgically remembered how he continued issuing visas through his train windows and how the refugees waved to him as they thanked him for their visas. Now, like them, he was trying to escape on the same route as they had taken and was possibly on the same train that they had ridden. He thought it rather ironic that he too was now caught up in a desperate situation similar to what the refugees had gone through. He also saw the irony in the fact that all these recollections were going through his mind while riding a train and trying to get back to Japan just as they had done. He wondered if anyone of them had successfully escaped.

Instead of a few days, they stayed in Odessa for about three weeks. This is where the Sugihara photos were confiscated. Due to Yukiko's persistence, the family photos were returned to her. Miraculously, among those photos were the two pictures of the people in the crowd. It took a period of almost three months for the family to travel through the frigid tundra of Siberia. They would stop for a short duration at small camps, but the cause for their real delay was the slowness of the train. Since the train was really a cargo train, they would stop and unload their cargo and wait for another engine to come by to continue to pull them on their journey to Vladivostok. In March of 1945, they finally arrived at a settlement called Nakhodka where Japanese soldiers were held. During their stay, they learned about the perilous state of the Japanese soldiers who were imprisoned there. They lived in very primitive conditions and had scant food. While they were there, Yukiko and her sister found a way to sneak over the soup that they were served, to the soldiers who greatly appreciated it. The family could not stomach the soup themselves so they secretly found a way to pass it on to the soldiers every day. Yukiko and her sister even made hand-rolled cigarettes and passed it through the barbed wire fences to the poor soldiers. The Japanese soldiers constantly lived under the fear that they would be soon sent to Siberia at any moment. Despite their dreary circumstances, like the German soldiers, they found ways to lessen the gloom of each day. One of them noticed that the Sugihara children still had their violins so they asked if they could borrow it for a concert. A few of the soldiers were accomplished players, so the family enjoyed one night of musical pleasure at Nakhodka.

Chiune was becoming concerned. Why were they staying in Nakhodka for such a long extended period of time? He was becoming very uneasy and imagining that they were checking him out. Not long after, one of the army guards in a unit began conversing with Chiune. He praised Chiune about his ability to speak Russian. During the course of their conversation, he brought up the fact that he had noticed Yukiko's beautiful Japanese kimono among their baggage. He let Chiune know that it would make his wife very happy if she could have a beautiful kimono. Chiune realized that the soldier was actually suggesting a possible bribe. In other words, release from Nakhodka in exchange for Yukiko's beautiful kimono. He related the incident to Yukiko. Although that was the last kimono that she had left, she told Chiune to tell him that in exchange for their release from Nakhodka, she would give his wife her kimono. Yukiko did not want to continue living in a state of constant uncertainty about whether or not Chiune would be taken away from them. She wanted the family to be released from their imprisonment as soon as possible.

That exchange did the trick and the Sugihara family was on their way to Japan, their homeland. They had been away from their country for ten years and their children did not know anything about Japan. They boarded what was described as a repatriation ship. These were the kind of ships that the soldiers in Nakhodka were hoping to board so that they could return to Japan instead of being sent to Siberia. Their vessel was a small Japanese ship named the Koan Maru. Aboard the ship, it was strange to hear everyone speaking Japanese, their native tongue. It was a short trip and the family arrived in Hakata Port on April of 1947. Their European Odyssey had lasted over ten years. They were happy to return.

PART V: ADVERSITY AND REDEMPTION (1946-1986)

THE RETURN

"A man travels the world over in search of what he needs and returns home to find it."
George Moore

As the family joyously stepped upon the soil of their Homeland, they realized that they had been away too long. Hiroki, the eldest son was full of excitement having had no recollection of Japan. He had heard stories about the country of his birth from his Aunt and was excited to discover that it was so different and new to him. As Yukiko and Chiune disembarked from their ship, they realized that they were virtually penniless. Most of their funds were still in Swiss banks. They decided to go to Yukiko's mother's home in Numazu because it was in a more convenient location for Chiune who was expecting to report to the Foreign Ministry in Tokyo as soon as they were settled. When they arrived in Numazu, they were disappointed to find that the home had been vacated. They finally located Yukiko's mother and family. They had left their home in Numazu in order to go to a safer place where they would not have to live in fear of being bombed by the Allies. The family had a tearful and joyful reunion. Since they had not received any word from them for many years, they had feared that something terrible might have happened to the family. The Japanese people endured great suffering from shortages in everything from food to housing. Anything that was available had to go to the men in the armed forces first. In a nation where land for agriculture, space for raising livestock, and natural resources were very scarce, it was a sad sight to see the deplorable conditions that they had to live under. Chiune Sugihara remembered well the sense of foreboding that he experienced when he first heard that Japan had attacked Pearl Harbor. Now he saw first hand how the people of his land were suffering from the deprivations that came with war. Food was scarce and their diet now was not much better than what they had lived on during their internment and journey back to Japan.

The children had some adjustments to make because their clothes were of European style and they looked strange and very foreign to the Japanese children in the neighborhood. The fact that the children still spoke in German to each other also kept them apart from the other Japanese children. Eventually, they adjusted very well and were speaking in Japanese as if they had spoken the language all of their lives. Special tutors were needed to help the children catch up to their grade level in reading and writing since they had not had formal Japanese schooling all the while they were in Europe.

Chiune was given three months to settle his family and expected to report back to the front office very soon. In the meantime, they were able to get their funds from the Swiss Bank. Chiune also decided that it was best for the family to live in their own home so he decided to go to Gifu, his ancestral home, to sell property that he owned there. With the funds that he received from the sale of his property, he bought a piece of land in Kugenuma. Earlier in the story, it was mentioned that Hiroki believed that his father chose to live in Kugenuma, because he had become familiar with that locale while visiting Hirota, Koki. Whatever the reason was that made Chiune choose to live there, he appeared to be quite familiar with that place and purchased land there to build his first home. Kugenuma was near Fujisawa City in Kanagawa Prefecture. It was a beautiful site near the Pacific Ocean. Building of their new home was started and the Sugihara family slowly adjusted to living in Japan. A few days before the three months period was up, Chiune received a letter from the Foreign Ministry instructing him to report to the Tokyo office.

THE "RESIGNATION"

"Thus ready for the way of life or death, I wait the sharpest blow."
William Shakespeare

On his way to reporting to his office for the first time since returning from Japan, he had hopes that the new government of Japan had learned from their experience from the war and was looking forward to new beginnings. He hoped that they were ready to shed their outdated bureaucratic standards and would move forward with an enlightened view of a more vital and democratic government. He dared to feel optimistic about whether he would be reprimanded for the "Incident in Lithuania." It was his belief that he was in the best position to serve his country because he was aware of the problems that loomed over relations with the Soviet Union. He felt that he had the capabilities to help to alleviate and resolve future problems with the Soviets. As he entered the office, he was met by Vice Foreign Minister Okazaki. The usual formalities and words were conveyed. Vice Minister Okazaki broached the subject of his future assignment. He stated that due to the downsizing of the Foreign Ministry department, Chiune's services would no longer be needed. He did not mention any future prospects or offer recommendations for other positions, which was the usual procedure. Although Chiune was prepared to pay the consequences of what he had done, he was still stunned to hear what he was told. Before leaving, he asked for further explanation about their decision and Okazaki brought up the topic of insubordination and related it to the "Incident in Lithuania." As he left the office, Chiune Sugihara experienced a feeling of great despair and disappointment. He realized that he was now facing the greatest challenge of his life.

When he returned to his home, Hiroki remembered that he was very pale and was speechless for a long period of time. Yukiko discerned what might have happened and finally broke the silence. He simply told her that he was asked to resign from the Japanese Foreign Ministry. Of course Yukiko was beside herself with anger and threatened to confront the vice Foreign Minister. Chiune reminded her that when they made the decision to issue visas, they had discussed the possibility of recriminations and had accepted that possibility back then. Therefore, he told her that he was ready to accept the consequences of what they had done and was putting it all behind him. He said that his focus was now on making plans about what he was going to do for their future. After a few days, when Yukiko had calmed down a bit, they discussed their current situation and they both agreed that despite what had happened, they still agreed that they would not have done anything differently. They both knew in their hearts that they had done the right thing.

This first indication that trends in their life were not going well was his "forced resignation." Soon after the first devastating blow, an even greater blow was dealt to Chiune and his family. Their youngest son, Haruki, came home from school not feeling well and went to rest in his bed. Very shortly after he had lain down,

Photo taken after funeral services for young Haruki who passed away at age 7.

he started to have severe bleeding from his nose. They called the doctor but there was nothing he could do to stop the flow of blood. Japan was suffering great shortages in everything and that also included medication. That night, young Haruki passed away at the young age of seven years. It was later diagnosed as a form of leukemia. Yukiko firmly believed that it was due to the lack of proper rest and nutrition that he lacked the immunity to fight off the disease. The whole family was devastated. Chiune seemed to suffer the greatest grief and for the longest period of time, he spent his time alone and hardly spoke a word to anyone. Following that tragedy, another blow struck. Aunt Setsuko became afflicted with toxic poisoning due to kidney malfunction during her pregnancy and died at childbirth. Setsuko had married one of Chiune's colleagues that she had met in Europe and had become pregnant with her first child when they returned to Japan. All of these series of tragedies was a real test of Chiune's true mettle. He spent several months grieving and allowed himself a time to heal. He realized that his family needed him and were depending on him. He needed time to get his mind in proper perspective, and he realized that he had not yet recovered completely from their European ordeal. After a few months, he was ready to tackle the challenges of making a living to provide for his family. He was never afraid of any kind of work, but the problem was how many people were willing to hire someone who was almost 48 years old. He was willing to try any kind of job that came his way. He worked as a tutor, a manager at a fabric store, and even spent a few days trying to sell light bulbs door to door. His career as a light bulb salesman was doomed to failure. He did not have the kind of skill to talk to strangers at their door while trying at the same time to convince them to buy his light bulbs. The family remembers well the boxes of light bulbs that were piled up in the house for quite a number of years. Hiroki always commented, "We never had to buy light bulbs in the Sugihara family." For a very short while he had a position working for the World Peace Foundation. The family could not remember what he did there. He even attempted being an entrepreneur like his father, Yoshimizu. He opened up a small concession where he sold small items such as pencils, notebooks, candy, small toys etc. He worked from early morning to late at night and it helped provide for some income for the family. The family also managed because of his meager earnings, and the few hundred dollars of retirement allowance that he received from the Foreign Ministry, helped to make ends meet. His first good job was for a trading company that specialized in selling fine fabrics and textiles. The owner, a Mr. Pombe', needed someone to translate for him. Mr. Pombe' spoke English and Russian so he needed someone who spoke both those languages as well as Japanese. Chiune was the perfect man for the job and he was hired. Unbeknownst to Mr. Pombe', who had been a leader of the Joint Distribution Committee, the group who helped finance the refugee's cost for their tickets, was the fact that Chiune was the person who was responsible for giving the refugees a chance to buy those tickets. When that fact was brought to the attention of the owner and managers of the shop about who Chiune was, he completely refused to discuss it with anyone.

His best and most significant job as far as the family was concerned was his job at the United States government run PX stores that was provided for the occupation forces. He was hired for his English speaking ability and was hired as a manager and translator. This job was of special significance to the Sugihara family because through the PX, Chiune was able to get rare food items not available to the general Japanese public. The family's main staple was potato. They ate sweet potatoes, regular potatoes, Japanese style potatoes, but it was always potatoes. Due to his job at the PX, he was able to occasionally bring home precious delicacies such as items like canned meat, canned fruit, and one day he even brought home a luxury item, a telephone. On some rare occasions when he had a chance to return to Yaotsu for short visits, he was able to bring home white rice which was considered a luxury food item. When the PX closed down, Chiune had to find other employment. The economy of Japan was beginning to improve and more jobs requiring his skills became available. His first significant job that reflected that there was a need for the skills that he had was his job for the NHK National TV Network. He was hired to work in the International Department for the Soviet Union. He was also able to work part time as an instructor at Nicholas Institute where he taught Russian. Their personal lives were becoming stabilized and at least they felt more comfortable about his job situation. Chiune no longer associated with his former colleagues because of certain unpleasant rumors that he discovered were being said about him. The groundless and insidious rumor was that he had profited from the Jewish refugees when he had issued those visas. Not one known survivor to this day has been known to make such an accusation. On the contrary, many of them even remarked that he did not accept anything. Most remember that he charged only two Lithuanian litas. When he had been asked to resign from the Foreign Ministry, he had vowed that he would put the past behind and so the fact of distancing himself from his past colleagues was part of this vow. It is not known how Chiune felt or what he thought when it was announced that his mentor, Hirota, Koki had been executed and had died by hanging in December of 1948. It can be presumed with a high degree of certainty that he mourned his death, but knew that he had lived well and had died valiantly.

Just about the time that he was beginning to accept the reality of the loss of his son, Haruki, Yukiko informed him that she was with child. She always knew that this child would be a boy because she remembered that before Haruki passed away, they had an unusual conversation. He had told his mother that he did not care if he died young because he wanted to be an angel in heaven. She was perturbed by what he had said and wondered where he got such a strange notion because they never discussed the topic of angels or any other biblical references. So she said to him, "Please don't talk like that because Mama would feel very sad if that happened." He then comforted her by saying, "Don't worry because I will come back to see you." Therefore, when their fourth son was born, she named him Nobuki, which meant Long Life. Yukiko also always regarded Nobuki as a kind of reincarnation of Haruki.

With the birth of a new son in 1951, Chiune was jubilant. It also seemed to set into motion many new beginnings for the family. Chiune's jobs offers were more frequent and they were jobs of a higher caliber. In 1952, he worked for Sanki Trade, as an executive. In 1954, the Japan Science and Technology agency hired him as a translator. As a translator there, the languages that he translated were for literary works in Russian, English, German and French. He also had an interesting project in which he translated commercial films. However, his first major job that required changes in his life again was when he accepted the position as an executive for the Kawakami Trading Company in Moscow. Yukiko was not encouraged to go with him because of his concern that she would not be happy living in the cold climate of Moscow and would get lonely there. Another concern was young Nobuki's education. He felt that it would be better for him to continue his education in Japan. His job at Kawakami Trading was to communicate with the Russians and to negotiate purchases of crude oil from the Soviets for Japanese fishing vessels. In actuality, he was representing the Association of Japan Fishermen. The president of the association at that time was Zenkoh Suzuki, who later became a Prime Minister of Japan. In 1964, the Kawakami Trading Company was sold and bought by the Chori Trading Company. They rehired Chiune as their executive and he was in charge of the department that exported sewing machines to the Soviet Union.

During this phase of his life while he lived away from his family, he usually visited them at least twice a year. The family always looked forward to his return and enjoyed receiving little gifts that he always brought back for them. It didn't take long for him to adjust to living in Moscow. He lived in a modest apartment at the Hotel Ukraine. As mentioned previously, he still maintained his frugal habits and tried to economize on his own expenses in order to send the rest of his salary to Yukiko and the family. In many ways, life in Moscow resembled his life in Harbin when he had been married to his Russian wife. Although he was aware of the fact that he was under surveillance by the KGB, he realized all foreigners were under some degree of scrutiny. He had also changed the spelling of his name to Sugiwara just as a safety measure. Living in Moscow also gave him opportunities to reacquaint himself with the Russian culture that he had learned to love in Harbin. He attended concerts, ballets, and became an avid fan of a popular singing group called the Darkdaks. He especially liked listening to their folk songs and romantic ballads. He tolerated temperatures like –30degrees very well. In fact, one of his favorite pastimes was to take solitary walks through the soundless snow covered birch forests in below freezing temperature. It was for him a cathartic experience because he said that during those solitary walks, "I felt that it helped to cleanse my mind."

Chiune did not lack for friends or a social life. Many of his former colleagues and former students were now also working in Moscow. When his son Hiroki paid him a visit in Moscow, he was pleased to see that his father had a group of former student followers that still called him Sensei (teacher). Even if they respectfully addressed

(left) A snapshot of Chiune taken in his room at the Hotel Ukraine (right) A photo of Chiune taken circa 1980, before his illness.

him as Sensei, their relationship with him evoked the feeling of an easy camaraderie. After a days work, it was not unusual for him to go out for a drink with his former students. Not only did he continue to be their mentor, but he was also helpful to them, because he found employment for many of his former students.

A Russian family that came to the United States in the 1980s, also recalled being very good friends with Chiune in Moscow. The husband and father of this family was a biological scientific doctor who had been working on a vaccine in Moscow contacted Chiune about an apparatus made in Japan that he was using to develop a vaccine. Because of some kind of technical problem with the apparatus, Chiune was called upon to act as an intermediary between the company that made the apparatus and the Russian doctor. Acting as an intermediary, he was able to help him solve the problem. As a result, he helped the doctor to complete his work on the vaccine that eventually saved many lives. Their collaboration led to a lasting friendship. The good doctor and Chiune both enjoyed the theater and the arts and they frequently attended concerts and many other cultural events together. The son of the doctor, who is currently a mathematical engineer in the United States, fondly remembers Chiune. He remembers him well because he shared his love of stamps with him and gave him many stamps from Japan. He also said that because Chiune spoke passionately about his love for his country and its culture, the young man who became a engineer also gained an interest and love for the culture of Japan. He felt that Chiune was the ultimate goodwill ambassador of Japan while he was in Moscow. It appears that Chiune personally continued assisting people who needed help.

THE REUNION

"In Life there are meetings which seem Like a fate."
Owen Meredith

It happened in 1968, during one of his visits home. Chiune received a call from the Israeli Embassy. A visitor, a Mr. Nishri, wanted to urgently meet him and wondered if Chiune could visit the embassy some time soon. Chiune was planning to return to Moscow very soon so he went the next day to the Israeli Embassy. Waiting at the embassy was a man who was overjoyed to see him. The first thing he asked him was, "Do you remember me?" Chiune could not recall who he was until he showed him one of the visas he had issued. Then it all came back to him. He realized that he was meeting for the first time, after 28 years, one of the refugees who had received his visa. Emotions ran high as they reminisced over what had happened during those desperate days in 1940. Chiune remembered him as one of the five representatives. As they continued their conversation, it was discovered that they had both been searching for one another. Chiune told him of his attempts to find out what might have happened to all the refugees, but was never able to get any information. However, he happened to leave his name and address at the Israeli Embassy in case any information came up. It happened that Mr. Nishri who was now an Attache' for the Israeli Embassy picked up on his name recently. He had been searching for him for the past several years but the Japanese information center could not provide any information. The Sugihara's wondered why that was so because there was a registry called the Kasumegaseki Registry that listed all former diplomats. Among the list, there were three Sugiharas, but only one who had served in Kaunas. Despite the fact that their search appeared to be fruitless after all those years, it was fate that they were destined to meet as they did that day and they rejoiced over their reunion.

When Chiune realized that most of the refugees that had received his visa had successfully escaped by first going through Russia to Vladivostok and finally reaching Japan safely, he was overjoyed. He was also told about the exorbitant increase in price of those tickets. To help pay for the fee of 200 USA dollars, organizations such as the JDC (Joint Distribution Committee) worked with JTB (Japan Travel Bureau) to insure safe passage through Russia. After all these years he had wondered about their fate, and dared not speculate what might have happened to them. That memorable day was the day that Chiune Sugihara really understood that the decision that he and Yukiko had made was without doubt, the only right thing to do. He also learned that some of the refugees who did not have all the proper documents were able to get them with the help of the Japanese Ambassador in Moscow. Ambassador Tatekawa, of Moscow had originally been a hard-liner who was inclined to strictly follow all the proper procedures before granting visas to the refugees who were trapped in Moscow. Later, he became more flexible when he became better apprised about the refugee problem, and helped some of the refugees to reach Japan safely. Another Sugihara colleague from Harbin was Acting Consul General Nei of Vladivostok who made the decision to allow the refugees to board ship to head for Tsuruga Port out of sympathy for their plight. Whether Chiune had any influence on this Consul due to their relationship at Harbin Gakuin, was never determined. These two men like Sugihara chose to commit to actions that demonstrated their sympathetic nature rather than choosing to be complete bystanders. When Sugihara suggested to the refugees before he left that he believed that there would be someone there that would help them, did he suspect that one or both of them would try to help? He was told that the majority of the refugees that did not have final destinations stayed in Kobe for several months and was eventually sent to Shanghai where they stayed until the end of the war.

Following the reunion of the two, the news about Sugihara's "Mission of Mercy" was covered in all the major newspapers. There were special reunion events and visits from dignitaries anxious to meet this newly discovered forgotten hero. Another reunion was organized and held at the Israeli Embassy and it was a memorable and tearful event for the many that attended. Sugihara continued his job in Moscow and tried to avoid any recognition when the excitement had subsided following the initial discovery about what he had done. However, when he was invited to visit Israel as a special guest, he accepted that invitation. By then his

During a visit to Israel as a special guest, Chiune met with Rabbi Zorach Warhaftig, Minister of Religious Affairs. Zorach Warhaftig is a recipient of Sugihara's visa. He described Chiune as an "Emissary of God"

youngest son Nobuki had accepted a scholarship offered to him to attend Hebrew University, so Chiune accepted the invitation because it was also an opportunity to visit his son. During his visit there, he had a reunion with Zorach Warhaftig, who was one of the five representatives at the Consulate. They had a wonderful meeting and Warhaftig described Chiune as an "Emissary of God." He was also given a tour of Yad Vashem, a special memorial of the Holocaust. There he went through the archives where all the names of the victims of the Holocaust were listed and also to the hall where the names of the Righteous Gentiles were engraved. Little did Chiune suspect that his name would be among them in the near future. He was moved when he saw the names of the 22 death camps engraved on the floor of the hall. It was a trip that he never regretted taking and always cherished the memory of his visit.

In 1976, Chiune began to notice symptoms that related to heart problems and decided to retire from his job and go back to live permanently in Japan. Due to economic setbacks suffered by the family, it was decided that they would sell their home in Kugenuma. They bought a more modest home in Kamakura, not far from Kugenuma. It was a location that was still close to the sea that Chiune had learned to love. Yukiko would frequently go for walks with him along the seashore while he used his cane to help keep his balance. One of the chores that he enjoyed was to putter in the garden and he seemed to take special delight in weeding. He was meticulous about getting rid of every bit of weed. He still enjoyed playing the piano and he had increased his repertoire from the Moonlight Sonata to one more favorite piece, "The Hand Maiden's Prayer." Whenever he was asked to be a guest for an interview on television, or asked by a reporter for an interview, he usually declined. He also spent hours organizing his papers and putting them in order. As his condition declined, he restricted his activities and usually stayed in his room. He still enjoyed his favorite snack that consisted of a rice dumpling covered with a sweet bean sauce. During one of his rare interviews, he did say the following, "I am just a simple and normal person who cherishes the fact that I found within myself, the courage that was needed at the time I needed it, to help those people who needed my help." He told a reporter that persisted in trying to get a reply from him that when people do something good, he hoped that they did it because it is the right thing to do, and not for any other ulterior motives. By 1984, he had suffered several heart attacks. During his illness, he never complained and only asked Yukiko to hold his hands before he fell asleep.

On January of 1985, the Jewish Community Center in Tokyo hosted a reception for soon to be Prime Minister of Israel, Yitzak Shamir. Prime Minister Nakasone of Japan, who was working towards building stronger ties with Israel, had invited him. Chiune was also invited as a special guest. His health had been in decline and although he had difficulty walking, he did attend this event and it was requested that he sit next to Israeli Ambassador to Japan, Ben Yohanon. This was the last public function that he was able to attend. In 1985, Chiune Sugihara was notified that he

In 1985, a reception was held at Tokyo's Jewish community center. The event was attended by Prime Minister Yitzak Shamir of Israel who is seated next to Chiune. Hiroki is standing to the left of the former prime minister. Yukiko is next to Chiune.

was chosen as the recipient of a most prestigious honor to be awarded by the Yad Vashem in Israel. He was selected as one of the "Righteous Among the Nations;" an award given to righteous gentiles. Because of his weakened condition, it was not possible for him to travel such a great distance. Yukiko and his eldest son, Hiroki went in his place to receive the honor. A special monument was also built for him in Jerusalem. Next to the monument was a cedar tree, the holiest of woods for the Jewish people because their first temple was built from cedar. But it also denoted the meaning of his name, cedar grove.

HIS PASSING

"Grant memory to us, and we lost nothing to death"
John Greenleaf Whittier

In July of 1986, Chiune's condition had become worse, so it was decided that he should be hospitalized. On July 31, the family visited him and when the doctor had assured them that he would be all right, they left for the day. However, later that day, he passed away quietly. Over 300 people attended his funeral. He received official condolences from the Israeli government. Many of those who attended his funeral were former colleagues who had worked with him in Moscow. Many of his friends and former students of Harbin Gakuin were also in attendance. His wife Yukiko, Hiroki and his family, Chiaki, and Nobuki paid their last respects, and he was laid to rest at Kamakura Cemetery.

Hiroki, his eldest son, spoke of his father in a way that only a son can know. For Hiroki and his brothers, their father was truly a parent that gave them unconditional love. He never criticized them harshly and accepted them for who they were and accepted what they did without criticism. Hiroki often believed that his father did not want to affect his children in the way his father had affected him when he had unintentionally imposed his will on him to become a doctor. He always had time to listen to them all and avoided being too critical of their opinions or ideas of what he thought of them. He also refrained from telling them about what he thought they should do if he was not asked. Hiroki remembered that his father was the one who woke up early each morning to prepare his breakfast when he was going to school. He was the one who celebrated his acceptance to a prestigious high school, Shonan School, in Kamakura, Kanagawa Prefecture, by presenting him with a gift of a stereo system that he had wanted for a long time. It was his father who helped him out of

The dedication ceremony for the opening of the Hill of Humanity in 1992. In the center are Hiroki Sugihara and Mrs. Yukiko Sugihara. To the far right is former Prime Minister Noboru Takeshita who helped finance the memorial. Mr. Ikami, standing on Hiroki's right was the driving force behind this project.

a financial difficulty that occurred in his life and affected the life of the whole family. He was the father who took a job in Moscow that separated him from his family; and sent most of his salary to his mother so that they would be well cared for financially. He was the father who was a quiet, gentle, and thoughtful person who never gossiped or spoke of others in a critical way. Hiroki's role model was his father. As a youngster, he remembered that he always watched his habits and how he conducted himself very carefully. He hoped that he would grow up to be as dignified and as kind as his father was. The fact that he had such a big impact on the lives of others was not ever fully understood until the discovery of his father by a survivor. At that point, the story of his rescue was revealed to the world. Within the family structure, it was accepted that he was the kind of person who was likely to be involved in situations where he would find ways to be helpful to others. It was behavior that was typical of a father like Chiune Sugihara that only a son could know and cherish.

In the year 2000, a plaque was placed in the Japanese Foreign Ministry office and was unveiled by Mrs. Yukiko Sugihara. It was a plaque that recognized Chiune Sugihara and his service to the Foreign Ministry. After the unveiling, Foreign Minister Yohei Kono, eloquently expressed the government's overdue appreciation from the Japanese people and government for Chiune Sugihara's act of humanitarian intervention.

(left) A memorial bust of Chiune Sugihara at the Hill of Humanity. (right) The Hill of Humanity, dedicated in 1992. It was a memorial inspired by the townspeople of his hometown in Yaotsu, Gifu Prefecture.

In his hometown of Yaotsu, in Gifu Prefecture, is a beautiful monument that honors his memory. It is on a hill and it is appropriately called the Hill of Humanity. The townspeople and town government proudly donated the property where the monument stands. The project was funded by former Prime Minister Noboru Takeshita, Taisei Construction Company, the late Mr. Takao Ikami, and Gifu Prefecture and Yaotsu Town. On the grounds of the monument, there is an informational museum visited by many people throughout the year.

Chiune Sugihara is remembered and honored by many. There are also those who are critical of him for his "insubordination." His reply to his critics was always, "History will be my judge." At Yad Vashem, there is an engraved inscription that says, "To Remember and Never Forget." It is estimated that over 100,000 individuals live today because they are recipients of his Gift. Chiune Sugihara's gift has become a living testimony through the lives of those who live today and has become a gift for the whole world as it shines brighter each day.

Yukiko Sugihara who is now 93 years old is living under the care of a nursing home as a result of a stroke. When asked about why she has spent the last ten years telling her family's story and about her husband, Chiune Sugihara, all over Japan and in places in the United States, her reply was simple. She stated, "If these stories bring about heightened awareness to young people of the past through our story, the hope is that when they hear our story and stories of others, mistakes will not be repeated."

Chiune Sugihara regarded life as man's most precious gift. He believed that all life should be appreciated, and regarded with respect and dignity.

APPENDIX

The following pages will update the readers about what happened to the survivors whose stories were chronicled in this biographical account of the Life and Times of Chiune Sugihara. The first survivor whose story was told is that of George Liebert. The following is an update about George and all the other survivors. It will include the story of how they managed to survive on another level. Bereft of most of their personal, material belongings and for the most part, virtually penniless, how did they meet the new challenges facing them? What were the mechanisms and behaviors that enabled them to gain a foothold in a foreign land? Miraculously, the four families in our stories all did. The stories of how they picked themselves up, adjusted and finally adapted to their new home is another amazing story. Their eventual accomplishment and their contribution to society is also a living testimony to Chiune Sugihara's Gift of Life. These stories also inherently have within them, lessons to be learned about what it took to change their lives, become mainstreamed into the fabric of a new environment, and to become Americans.

George Liebert: George is still very much alive and well. I consider him a living icon because he is a perfect blend of the old and the new. When you meet George, you meet the finest of what real gentlemen were like at the beginning of the century as well as someone that is in charge and understands what it is all about in today's world. He is well mannered, a learned man of the world, and even a dashing figure who wears his French beret jauntily on his head. He can probably charm anyone when he says something in fluent Russian, or quotes poetry in French, and even sing songs to you in German.

George is a true survivor. He has never forgotten what he experienced while trying to escape the Nazi's drive to rid Europe of all Jews. Each day, he is thankful for his life in the United States. It is not an option for George to feel unappreciative for each day he wakes up in the morning. When he first landed on United States soil, he was one of those who was virtually penniless. At first he managed to survive taking on small jobs. He was not afraid to take any opportunity that came his way so that he could begin to start his life anew. He even learned how to repair shoes. To this day he still has a shoe repair kit in his very comfortable apartment near Central Park. He can boast that his shoes could last for decades. Although

George Liebert standing with his friend and attorney, Joe Salomon

he was trained to be a chemical engineer at the University of Bordeau, he chose to take on more unique and unusual ways to insure that his life would eventually become more comfortable and stable. One of the unusual jobs he undertook and was very successful with was as an antique dealer. He successfully bought and sold European antiques in the United States and Europe. Coming from a very affluent family who owned a glass factory in Krakow, he was very familiar with fine things. He had incredible adventures in the jungles of South America bringing two Cadillac cars and risking all the dangers just to deliver those two cars for a client who had ordered them. While there, he learned about semi precious stones and succeeded and making a profit buying and selling them. But his biggest coup was when he had an idea of investing in land and building co-op apartments. The demand for housing was there and George was again at the right place and at the right time because his investments made him a very comfortable man. He was not afraid to take chances, and when he did, he took extra thought and measures that assured success for his endeavors. His ability to look for opportunities and to take them when they appeared was how he survived the Holocaust. These very same traits helped him to adjust and to be a survivor in his new life.

George never got married because he was very busy engaged in the business of succeeding in his chosen fields of employment during each endeavor. He also was committed to caring for his mother when she arrived from Poland in 1960. He was a devoted son and took care of her until her death. Today, George is generous to causes he believes in. He also helps families from his native Poland who find themselves in difficulties and provides guidance and financial help to those he believes in and chooses to help. He is a happy person and there is never a dull moment when you are around George. He travels easily anywhere in New York and knows all the bus and subway routes and gets around like a person in his early 70s. He also has a collection of jokes that are all original "George Jokes." Each of his jokes is numbered and he can immediately tell the joke when a number is given that triggers his memory about a given joke by their numbers. One of his jokes is reminiscent of the days when the Refugees were in fear of being imprisoned by the Russians. George will say, Stalin was the best dentist in the world because he succeeded in pulling teeth through people's noses." This alludes to the fact that while in Russia, no one dared open one's mouth to say anything for fear of being arrested.

When George speaks about Sugihara, he always says, "He was a very unique person and there are not many people like him. He just saved people because he was a good man and he did not even ask for any money when he issued the visas." George also remembers that as the train pulled away carrying Chiune back to Berlin, he yelled to him and said, "Sugihara, we will never forget you!" George has kept his word because he has not forgotten and vividly remembers that day in Kaunas, Lithuania, on July 27, 1940, waiting to get his visa.

Rabbi Samuel Graudenz: When you first meet Rabbi Graudenz, he appears at first glance to be a stern man. However, it does not take long before one realizes that he is a very sweet and kind man with a tendency to display a mischievous sense of humor. It was this kind of sense of humor and faith in the goodness of man that sustained him during the dark days of the Holocaust. His relationship with Zorach Warhaftig and their contributions to urge the refugees to maintain hope and perseverance to reach Eretz Yisrael is an inspiration that should not be forgotten. He is staunchly honest and one would never doubt his every word to be true. He never compromises with the truth. His incredible story about the barter of his violin personifies his life. His life has always been unique from the time that he was sent to live in an orphanage to the present day. For example, when he first met his wife, Ruth Eva Damm in Shanghai, he was 27 and she was 151/2 years. Although quite young, Eva, as she was called, took the responsibility to care for the newborn son of a Jewish family who was a family friend in Shanghai. The family that Eva was helping, Lottie and Joe Tugendhaft, were also friends of Rabbi Graudenz. They were well aware of the fact that Samuel Greudenz was engaged to Regina Grabovnik, who had also grown up in the same orphanage with Samuel. However, Regina and Samuel were separated when they were caught up by the Germans and ordered on a "forced march" to a train station. The Tugendhafts believed that Regina most probably had not "made it out." Because they believed that Regina was no longer alive, they introduced Eva to Samuel. With his usual candor and fidelity, he told Eva that he was still engaged to Regina and could not commit to anyone else until he was able to confirm that Regina was murdered by

Rabbi Samuel Graudenz at a opening of a Sugihara photo exhibit sponsored by Union Bank of California and the Japanese Consul General's office of San Francisco. (left to right) CEO of Union Bank of CA, former CG, Tanaka; Rabbi Graudenz; President of VfLF, Dr. Ben Lesin; Chairperson of VfLF, Anne Akabori.

the Germans. After the war, Samuel inquired with the Red Cross about Regina as a missing person. Through records of her entry date into Auschwitz and the number tattooed on her arms, it was confirmed that she had been murdered in a gas chamber.

After the war, on December of 1946, Samuel and Eva boarded a US troop transport ship to finally leave Shanghai. Accompanying them were Eva's mother, Leonie and brother, Peter. Being confined in the cargo hold, it was an uncomfortable trip made worse because of seasickness. Before they had embarked upon the trip, they had already been engaged. The trip took about three weeks before they landed in San Francisco. From there, they traveled by train to New York because of the possibility that Eva's mother's sister would sponsor them. Despite some problems that existed because the sisters did not get along, they finally received their sponsorship and were allowed to live in the United States. It was difficult to find employment and Eva immediately took the opportunity to live with a family to care for their children. Samuel shared a room with another refugee in a rooming house and took any job that was found and offered by a Jewish organization that helped refugees find jobs. Eventually, they returned to the West Coast and settled in Seattle, Washington. They lived there until 1963 when they moved to the Bay Area. While in Seattle, Rabbi Graudenz founded the Seattle Hebrew Day School that enrolled children from kindergarten to 9th grade. They also started their family and had four children. All of them were born in Seattle. They were Jack (1948), Debby (1951), Judi (1956), and Becky (1958). All of their names were biblical names so their formal names were Jacob, Deborah, Judith, and Rebecca.

After moving to the Bay Area, Rabbi Graudenz continued his work in Jewish education first in Oakland, and later, in San Francisco. In 1968, he was offered the pulpit at Congregation Beth Shalom, a Conservative congregation in Modesto, California. During those years, he also worked on his day off as prison chaplain at Deuel Vocational Institute near Modesto. He was well liked by the inmates and on several occasions, they protected him during some riots that erupted there. When he retired from his Congregation at age 75, he continued to work one day a week at Deuel. After his retirement, he became the rabbi emeritus there. He also extended his work in prison institutions by working one day a week at the Women's Facility in Stockton and another day at Sierra Conservation Center in the foothills of Northern California. Despite the fact that he was considered legally blind, due to macular degeneration, he continued his work at the prisons for two more years until age 82. Eva was also committed to helping others. Eva became a volunteer at a local hospital and served twice as president of the volunteer association. Following surgery for pulmonary embolism, she passed away at the hospital that she had served on for many years as a volunteer.

Both Samuel and Eva Graudenz have succeeded in passing on the legacy of helping others to their children. All of their children are involved in good works that help those in need. For example, Jack the eldest, has lived in Israel since 1983. Besides raising their own three children, they have adopted five children. Four of those adopted children have Down's Syndrome. Debby is active in her community in Albany, California, with her son and husband. She is involved in creating programs and services to help Jewish families with disabilities as the coordinator of the Disability Services at Jewish Family and Children's Services of the East Bay. She also oversees the care of her father who is living in an assisted living facility in San Francisco. She is a devoted daughter who regularly visits her father and takes care that all of his needs are met. Her sister, Judi lives in Granite Bay, California and is a mortgage banker and is actively engaged in helping others less fortunate than herself. As a teacher in Central California, Becky Graudenz specializes in working with non-English speakers. Personally and through their children, both Rabbi Graudenz and his wife have succeeded in continuing the legacy of helping others through their adult offsprings. As Rabbi Graudenz has repeatedly said whenever he was invited to address groups, "Had it not been for Sugihara, I would not be here today." We can also say that, "Had it not been for Sugihara, the Graudenz Family would not be here to continue their contributions towards helping others." Through families like the Graudenz family, the legacy of Chine Sugihara shines more brightly each day.

The Melamdovich Family: The saying that, "an apple does not fall far from its tree," is most appropriate when it comes to describing Isaac and his son Leo. Isaac was a radical, a visionary, an educator, a revolutionary, instinctive, and he had the courage to follow his heart and mind. He was all of this rolled up into one person. His son Leo, very early in life, showed that he was also endowed with all of that and had something more. He had patience, the ability to listen, and to value what others thought; characteristics that he most probably learned by observing his mother. With such a formidable array of positive characteristics, the forecast for his future was propitious

When the Melamdovich Family finally arrived in the United States, they were blessed because there were relatives who welcomed them warmly and joyfully. Unlike many of the refugees, they already had a support group waiting for them. They lived in New York for a short time. While Leo and his parents adjusted to a new environment, they also learned about the wonders of living in a diverse society such as New York. In 1941, Isaac and Faygl were offered permanent positions at the Sholom Aleichem Folks Institute schools of Chicago. It was a purely secular school that emphasized the arts and theater, literature, and culture of Yiddish ethnicity and heritage. The emphasis was on academics and the school maintained a policy of being apolitical and a non-religious one. Even in America, Isaac and Faygl Melamdovich remained staunch advocates of maintaining and preserving Yiddish culture. Isaac eventually became a principal and the chief operating officer of the school. In the meantime, young Leo went through the adjustments and travails of familiarizing himself with his new home and environment. Because of his parent's determination that he would not lose his Yiddish identity, they continued to speak in the pure unadulterated Yiddish language at home. This was at best a big challenge because that language in the United States had become anglicized and infected with colloquialisms, and usage that came from different regions of Europe. He also was encouraged by his parents to get involved in Yiddish Theater where he excelled because he had a natural dramatic flair. His forte was in recitation of poetry and soliloquy. This experience gave young Leo thoughts of a career in the theater. His practical parents discouraged this idea and encouraged him to pursue what they considered a more stable occupation, like being a doctor or lawyer. However, Leo's experience with the theater eventually became a useful and effective tool later in his life. Leo eventually completed his higher education in law, but he soon realized it was a career that could not fulfill his mental and emotional needs. He realized that his character demanded a profession that was more creative, innovative and dynamic.

Leo had been exposed to the commodities market earlier in his life while still a college student. Although his parents helped him with his college expenses, he was always strapped for more funds and was consistently faced with financial pressures. One of his best and oldest friends, Meyer Seltzer, knowing about his predicament called him one day about a lead he had heard about concerning a job that would fit into the time slot that he had between class hours at John Marshall Law school.

It was a job offered by Merrill, Lynch, Pierce, Fenner and Bean, a brokerage firm that sold stocks, bonds and commodities. Unknown to Leo at the time, his initial exposure to a world that was entirely foreign to him, was to become the driving force in his life. It would catapult him to become one of the leaders in the financial community.

Discovering that a career in law was somehow not fulfilling and challenging for him, Leo decided to take a big risk in his life, when he abandoned his reliable law business. He made the decision to enter the commodities market full time. While engaged in his law practice, he had also been actively engaged in commodities trading at the CME (Chicago Mercantile Exchange) or the Merc. He eventually realized that trying to do both things, to practice law and to trade in commodities, was untenable. He understood that to become really successful, he had to make a choice. Despite the fact that trading in commodities presented far greater risks as well as the disapproval of his father, Leo followed his heart and probably his instincts, and chose the riskier option. That decision was a pivotal point in his personal life. The decision also affected and influenced the commodities market as well. Due to Leo Melamed's vision, organizational skills, real understanding about what the market really was about, and his character, he made today's futures market an integral, valid, legitimately accepted, and respected institution that it has become worldwide. The key ingredient that enabled Leo to be the one person to meet the challenges of revolutionizing this institution was his character. Leo always believed that important things did not happen as a result of a whimsical stroke of luck, but was a product of those involved. And the special ingredient needed to reach those goals was the involved individual's character. Leo had the character to launch this revolutionary change, and he had the perseverance and knowledge to carry it through. Without doubt, Leo and his contributions can be considered as another great living testimony of Sugihara's Gift of Life.

Leo's accomplishments are numerous. It is appropriate to say that he fits the description as being a "Man of All Seasons of the 21st Century." He is an accomplished actor, a respected writer of business education, but also a science fiction author. Among the minor cultures within our society, he is ranked as a top bridge player and is even ranked as a formidable opponent in the game of ping-pong. His educational innovations in the business world are worldwide and highly respected by the business community. In fact, his books and writings are used as adopted texts in Japanese business schools. He continues to be actively involved and contributes to YIVO, an organization that maintains and preserves Yiddish culture, history and literature. He was appointed to be a director of the Holocaust Memorial Museum in Washington D. C. by President George Bush in 1992. There, he was instrumental in reviving Elie Wiesel's goal to establish a permanent Committee of Conscience at the Museum. After twelve years since the inception of the idea, on June of 1995, with Leo's leadership, it successfully became a reality and a permanent instrument of the Museum.

His innovations at the CME were revolutionary. An example was the creation and implementation of a public trust for the purpose of protecting customer funds, by insuring that no clearing firm defaulted, was a first in the futures exchange. By pushing for the involvement of the government or federal regulation, he was able to raise the standard and level of credibility of the futures market, thus insuring integrity within the system. In order to keep up with change and continued growth, he was at the forefront of introducing educational booklets as marketing tools that was eventually adopted by every exchange. It was one of Leo's important legacies. He understood that to become comfortable with the status quo was a sure recipe for eventual decline. He knew that change was a given. It was especially evident in fast-paced financial institutions where the dynamics was dependent on change every millisecond. Even though he understood that change was inevitable, he also realized the necessity of respecting one's roots. As difficult as it was to incorporate change, Leo had the conviction and organizational skills to make it happen. He clearly understood that being able to anticipate change was a key to survival. Under his guidance, the CME started from eggs and onions, to cattle and other commodities, and continued into financial futures. He changed the CME from a domestic to an international entity; from "open outcry" to a global electronic automated transaction system named Globex. Where once the monetary standard was based on gold priced at $35 an ounce, he introduced the concept of utilizing the currency market and foreign exchange. In order to survive and become a respected financial institution, he realized that CME must be built upon a base of a strong and stable administration. It also had to have the ability to expand its membership base, increase and diversify product line, enlarge the size of the working environment so that it's physical growth was consistent with growth of their financial market. Leo also emphasized that in order to stabilize it all, it was important to organize an effective and reliable support group. When Leo "really retired" in 1991, after many previous attempts to do so, the Chicago Tribune wrote in their editorial, "Leo Melamed, Father of Financial Futures."

Like his father, Isaac, Leo is definitely a survivor. He chose to work in a kind of world that posed great challenges. He met those challenges with the same kind of focus, perseverance, patience and energy, as did his father Isaac who managed to always keep one step ahead of his pursuers. Leo's ability to maintain a great sense of humor during some major disasters , enabled him to keep his cool and to persevere in the face of insurmountable obstacles. Like his father, he too had a vision, the fortitude, courage and tenacity to accomplish most of all his goals. As a parent of three children, his parents provided him with the best role model of good parenthood. Leo was blessed to have a wife who had all the characteristics necessary to support and understand a person as unique and committed to his profession as he was. Together, they raised three independent and interesting children, who are pursuing their own individual dreams. Their oldest and only daughter, Idelle, is a brilliant attorney by profession. She has presently chosen to be a mother and homemaker for her four children. Taking advantage of the opportunity of not being a working parent, she is presently expanding her horizons by studying library science. The next oldest in the family is Jordan, who is involved in the film making industry and is a movie director. It would be interesting to someday see a block buster film made by Jordan about his father whose life has been quite an amazing one. Finally, the youngest is David, who is a trader in the futures market. It would not be surprising if he would also make a mark in that industry someday.

From the family of Isaac Melamdovich, we now have eight Sugihara survivors. Each of them holds a promise for the future. Leo is definitely still in the game and it is a sure bet that he has some innovative and exciting ideas for the future. His depth of understanding about the market and about the international scene makes him an invaluable source for guiding and determining how to anticipate and to meet the challenges of the great changes that are coming and are even upon us. Leo is still in good physical shape and appears to be as every bit as active and vigorous as he was when he decided to "retire." Judging from his track record, it can almost be guaranteed that we have not heard the last of Liebl Melamdovich, better known as Leo Melamed.

The Descendants of the Salomon Brothers, Rick and Joe Salomon are cousins. Rick was the only son of Bernard or Boruch Szmul Salomon, as listed on Sugihara's list. He was the elder of two brothers who survived because they had received Sugihara visas. Joe Salomon is one of the three children of Abram, Ber-

(left to right) Hiroki Sugihara with Idelle, daughter of Leo, and Leo Melamed in 1998. Hiroki and Leo were guest speakers at Chicago's Righteous Ave. Ceremony

nard's younger brother. The story of how the two brothers eventually receive their priceless documents that enabled them to survive, was pieced together by information gathered by both Rick and Joe Salomon. Being direct descendants of the survivors, the information is considered, at best, second hand information. However, certain essential facts cannot be denied. It is understood that by utilizing intelligence, common sense, and intuition, they were counted as survivors, and did not become a part of the over six million Jews who were slaughtered and murdered by the armies of Hitler and Stalin during the Holocaust of WWII.

After the two brothers were given their first passage to freedom via the Sugihara/Zwartendijk visas, they took approximately two months to make preparations and get the proper documents to go through Russia. After reaching Moscow, they had to cross Siberia via the Trans-Siberian Railroad during the severest months of the year. By October, the winds coming from the arctic were in full force, and temperatures readily dropped to double digit minus degrees. The brothers most likely experienced the notoriously frigid Russian winter as they crossed the Siberian Steppes. They finally arrived in Vladivostok, the gateway to the Far East. They stayed in Vladivostok for about a month as they awaited passage to board a ship that would take them to Japan. It is indicated that they were in the group that reached Tsuruga Port in November of 1941. As it was for the majority of the refugees that did not have sponsorship to continue on their journey to a haven of safety, they were eventually shipped to Shanghai and placed into the Hong Kew district. This was the part of Shanghai that was under the jurisdiction of the Japanese military. Some of the refugees remember instances of harsh treatment and lack of proper living facilities, but when the alternative circumstances were considered, they were grateful to be alive and to live without fear of being imprisoned and eventually killed. The Foreign Ministry in fact refused Ribbentrop to return the refugees back to Germany when he requested it. Japan's reply was that they did not want to participate in the mass murder of innocent people based on their ethnicity, nationality or religion. The brothers did not remain in Shanghai like the majority of the refugees. Records indicate that they arrived in Calcutta, India by October of 1941.

The ingenuity of the Salomon brothers is quite evident when it was revealed that they had acquired several visas from different Consulates. From their recent past experience, they learned about, and fully understood the intrinsic value and life saving potential that having a visa provided. Rick recounts that his father had acquired a visa from the Bolivian Consulate, an Argentinian visa, and a Dominican Republic visa when he was in Calcutta. There is also record of a British visa to Palestine that was issued in Kobe. Along with the British document, he also was able to get another British transit visa to travel through India and Ceylon in Kobe. Bernard must have found a way to go to Tokyo from Kobe because he also received an Egyptian visa in Tokyo. The Salomon brother's determination to escape and to begin a new life is evidenced by the fact that they rarely missed any opportunity to get any visa in order to insure that they would somehow reach Palestine. When the Suez Canal was closed due to the war raging all over Europe and the Pacific Theater, their hopes of going to Palestine were dashed. As the true survivor that he was, Bernard resigned himself to do what he could and found employment in Calcutta, India as an accountant for a leather tannery. While there, he showed his commitment to Jewish causes by being a writer for a Jewish periodical in Calcutta; He also continued with his employment as an accountant.

Bernard waited out the war in Calcutta for six years. After the war, he was finally able to immigrate to the United States instead of going to Palestine. He was quick to acquire another job as an accountant in the United States. In 1948, he met Rick's mother and soon after they were married, he opened up his own business. Unfortunately, one and a half years after Rick was born, he passed away from heart disease. Due to the effects of a series of heart attacks and a stroke, he could not speak. However, he did know that he had a descendant, Rick, who insure the continuation of his family.

The poignancy in the story of Bernard Salomon is that after undergoing the hazards of imprisonment, evading capture, and relentlessly pursuing a ticket to freedom and succeeding, he did not get to know his only son, Rick. Rick is the kind of son that any father would be proud to point out and say, "That's my son." Because Rick cared about his identity and wanted to know more about his father and grandparents and further down his family tree, it lead to his interest in the Sugihara story. Rick realized that had his father not made it safely to the United States, he would not have ever met his mother, and therefore, he would not have ever existed. Rick is someone who really appreciates life and is proud and gratified that because his father was able to escape from Poland and Lithuania, he now has a beautiful family that he is thankful for every day.

A beautiful part of this poignant story is that much of the evidence seems to point to the fact that Rick truly embodies all the positive characteristics of his father, Bernard. It was Bernard who stayed as long as possible in Poland being the responsible son that he was, and barely escaped with his life to Vilnius. Rick, like his father, has the same sense of responsibility and is a loving, caring and nurturing parent. It is obvious that his father was quite an intelligent person because his survival was not a product of pure luck, but a combination of daring, calculation and perceptiveness. Rick has each of those characteristics and it is illustrated by the success of his thriving business. He is CEO of a highly successful consulting and management firm that advises many Fortune 500 companies. In other words, huge corporations and multinational companies go to Rick for advice and consultation about how to optimize and utilize their corporate earnings. His accounting ability and a certain kind of perceptiveness that Rick exemplifies is very reminiscent of his father's abilities.

Rick Salomon with his wife, Jaqueline, clockwise, his son, Mark, and daughter, Eve.

Bernard's family obviously realized the value of education. It is apparent by the fact that he was educated to be an accountant and was capable of writing articles for a newspaper. His brother, Abram, was also a graduate of the University of Warsaw and had successfully completed his education to be an attorney. Rick continues the family tradition of regarding education as a priority. His educational resume includes the University of Chicago, School of Law and Harvard Law School. When he received the prestigious Watson Fellowship, he went to study the criminal justice systems in Scandinavia and Eastern Europe. Before he began his career as CEO of his present position, he also clerked for a federal judge before becoming an associate and later a partner in an international law firm. Rick also carries on the tradition of education with his children. His two beautiful children, Mark (15), and Eve (14), both excel academically and are accomplished in extra-curricular activities. Mark plays in his school concert band and shows his versatility by playing both the trumpet and euphonium. Eve is a talented tap dancer as well as a basketball player. Like her grandfather, Bernard, who probably enjoyed writing, she also enjoys creative writing.

Besides his impeccable professional and educational credentials, some of Rick's other talents that I was not aware of, was brought to my attention by his cousin Joe. I realized then that Rick was a true "savant." His cousin Joe informed me that Rick was capable of playing the piano like a virtuoso pianist. Not only does he appreciate and collect fine art, he is also on the level of a professional in sport activities. His skill in playing pool, I am told, would qualify him to be a very successful pool shark. His tennis playing skills puts him among the ranks of the pros, and it is a common occurrence for him to be invited to play with professional players during weekend matches. Rick's physical fitness belies the fact that he is in his early 50s. Bernard Salomon would have indeed been very proud that he had a son like Rick who continues the family line.

Both Rick and his charming wife, Jaqueline, are very active in the Glencoe, Illinois community. Jaqui, as she prefers to be called, is a former junior high school history teacher and was also a library science major. She is a busy homemaker and also helps Rick from her home. Rick's involvement in community activities includes being a guest speaker to many Holocaust events. He always welcomes the opportunity to share his father's story of how he survived the Holocaust whenever there is a Sugihara event. For example, he was a keynote speaker in October, 2004, during the Anti-Defamation League Conference in Washington D. C. There, he addressed hundreds of students who were especially invited for the event because they participated in a Sugihara essay contest. Rick and his family participate in their synagogue activities and Rick has an active leadership role there. He is senior cabinet member of the Make-A-Wish Foundation of Illinois. Both of his children, Mark and Eve have also participated by helping with fund raising activities for Make-A-Wish Foundation as well as other organizations. Rick is committed to honoring and remembering the legacy of those individuals like Sugihara because he personally realizes its significance. He understands clearly that if there were not people like Chiune Sugihara, he and thousands of others would not exist today.

Joe Salomon's father, Abram, chose to go in a different direction when he left Calcutta. He went down south, to Australia. There he met his wife, and it was where their first born son, Joe was born in Melbourne, Australia. While still a youngster, the family immigrated to the United States. Abram Salomon had two more children after Joe. They were Adina and the youngest, B. Amir. Amir became his uncle's namesake when his father, Abram, named him B. Amir. The B stood for Bernard. Abram adjusted to life in the United States and continued as a practicing attorney. He also remained active and involved with activities of

(top) Joe Salomon as a child with his mother, and father, Abram Salomon

the Zionist movement. He took over the responsibilities of many Jewish organizations by taking on leadership positions. For example, he was Executive Vice President of the Jewish National Fund of America.

Joe is a very successful attorney himself, practicing in New York. His office is located right above the site of the former twin towers and offers spectacular views of New York. His sister, Adina, is an interior designer, and B. Amir is a successful radiologist practicing in Summit, New York. In fact, Adina's daughter was recently accepted to MIT; it is quite an accomplishment in today's competitive world. Every member of the Salomon family, both that of Bernard's and Abram's have succeeded and keeping up the tradition of appreciating the value of a good education and each of them are accomplished in their field. Joe and each of his siblings have two children each. One of Joe's daughters, Lisa, just recently had a son named, Henry Jacob Pollock. Henry would have been Abram's first grandchild.

Joe is a very affable and youthful grandfather. He also shares common qualities with his father. Abram, like his father, appears to have been the outgoing one of the family and retained a strong personal presence throughout his life. Joe is the kind of attorney that one could entrust with private and personal business. In fact, many of his clients can be counted to be among those who were rescued by Sugihara. George Liebert is also one of his clients. They have become very good friends as a result of finding out about all the family connections that they both shared. He expressed his appreciation of the significance of Sugihara's deed when he said, "As one of the progeny of the Sugihara survivors, it is easy to think of how many lives have been...and will continue to be...enabled as a result of his actions. It also puts into overwhelming perspective how many lives, and future lives, were preempted by the annihilation of over 6,000,000 Jews."

Today, because Bernard and Abram Salomon survived, there are presently, thirteen direct descendants of the Salomon Family of Mlava, Poland. Individually, each of them is contributing to our society in good and helpful ways. Each of them is a unique and beautiful human being. There could be no better gift to the world than the great potential these lives can hold for the betterment of mankind. The legacy of the Gift of Life is indeed a precious one. It makes everyone winners, as the recipients of Sugihara's gift continue to live with appreciation, and endeavor to show their thanks by simply living good and decent lives; they illustrate why Chiune Sugihara always maintained, that man's greatest gift is LIFE.